The Millionaire Employee

Investment Guide

HOW TO INVEST YOUR WAY TO A MILLION DOLLARS WHILE WORKING FOR A PAYCHECK

Dr. ROGER SMITH

**Author of *Becoming the Millionaire Employee*
and *Advice Written on the Back of a Business Card***

M

Modelbenders Press

The Millionaire Employee Investment Guide: How to Invest Your Way to a Million Dollars While Working for a Paycheck

Modelbenders Press books may be purchased for business and promotional use or for special sales. For information, please contact the publisher.

PRINTED IN THE UNITED STATES OF AMERICA

Visit our web site at www.millionaireemployee.com

Designed by Adina Cucicov at Flamingo Designs

The Library of Congress has cataloged the paperback edition as follows:

Smith, Roger
    The Millionaire Employee Investment Guide: How to Invest Your Way to a Million Dollars While Working for a Paycheck
    Roger Smith. – 1st ed.
    1. Investing   2. Career Management   3. Self-Help   4. Millionaire Behavior
    I. Roger Smith   II. Title

ISBN-13: 978-0-9843993-0-7
ISBN-10: 0-9843993-0-5

Table of Contents

Foreword..5
Chapter 1: The Millionaire Investment Plan..7
    Your Investing Plan...8
    The Millionaire Employee Plan...11
    Millionaire Employee Investor..25
Chapter 2: The Piggy Bank...27
    Money in the Mattress...29
    Burglars...32
    No Interest Earned in the Mattress...32
Chapter 3: The Big Bank...35
    Bank Accounts...41
    Interest Rates...41
    Checking Accounts..46
    Savings Accounts...48
    Certificates of Deposit...49
    Conduit to Bigger Investing..50
Chapter 4: The Wide World of Investing..51
    Stocks..53
    Bonds..55
    Real Estate...57
    Precious Metals..59
    Collectibles..60
    Mutual Funds..61
    Derivatives...62
    Summary..63
Chapter 5: Patterns of Investments..65
    Consumer Goods...65
    Real Estate...70
    Start a Business..74
    Stock Market...76
    Bonds..78
Chapter 6: Wading In..81
    How to Start..83
    Cycle Warning...86
    Depression Investing...90

Big Deal..91
Choosing Your Investments 92
Investing Experience..93
Chapter 7: Entry Level... Your First Three Years................................95
Getting Away from the Credit Card...97
Starting to Invest..98
401(k) 99
IRA...102
Savings...105
Stock Brokerage Account...107
Bonds...113
Beginning Real Estate 113
Summary 117
Chapter 8: Intermediate Investing in Stocks... Three to Ten Years.....119
Stocks vs. Other Alternatives...121
You Lucky Genius...121
In the Pits..123
Select an Industry..125
Investing in Your Profession..128
Outside Interests..130
Pros vs. Amateurs 131
When to Start...133
Selecting a Company to Invest In..134
Learn Before You Leap...135
Getting Educated...136
How much should you pay? 139
Value Investors 144
Growth Investor...145
Which Are You? 146
Chapter 9: Investment Styles of the Rich and Famous.......................147
Peter Lynch, One Up on Wall Street...148
Roger Smith, Becoming the Millionaire Employee...........................149
Michael Thomsett, Winning with Options..151
Christopher Browne, The Little Book of Value Investing 153
Warren Buffet, from The Warren Buffet Way by Robert Hagstrom.....163
Jim Cramer, Mad Money..171

Chapter 10: Mathematical Approaches...177
    Phil Towne, Rule #1 Investor 177
    James Stewart, Common Sense...185
Chapter 11: Intermediate Alternatives... Three to Ten Years........189
    International Stocks...189
    Prepaid College Tuition...191
    Bonds...192
    Real Estate..199
    Collectibles...204
Chapter 12: Experienced Investing... Over 10 Years.....................209
    Options..210
    Options Strategies..218
    Tax-Free Bonds...220
    Professional Investing..221
Chapter 13: Winning and Losing...223
    Losing Money...224
    Examine Yourself..227
    Diversification..230
Chapter 14: Saving to Spend...233
    College Tuition..238
    Vacation..240
    Automobile and Other Future Purchases................................240
    Down Payment for a Home..241
    Saving to Start a Business..242
    Downright Losses...243
Chapter 15: Where Do We Go From Here?......................................253
    Accountant...255
    Family Lawyer..255
    Will...256
    Estate Management Guide...257
    Conservator..258
    Living Trust..259
    Life Has Been Good...260
Chapter 16: Getting and Staying Educated.....................................263
    Books..264
    Periodicals 267
    Web Sites..268

Foreword

This is the investment companion to *Becoming the Millionaire Employee*. Both books are targeted at people eager to become wealthy, even though they know that they will be working for a company, university, or government agency their entire lives. Not everyone can become an investment banker, professional basketball player, or fast-growing entrepreneur. Most people spend their careers happily working for large organizations and are quite satisfied with the work they are doing. There is no reason that this type of career should prevent you from becoming wealthy.

Young professionals starting their first job out of college are the best candidates for the advice in this book. They have the most time to put the advice into practice and begin building their wealth early in their lives. However, millions of mid-career professionals realize that they do not have a plan for becoming wealthy either, or they never really believed they could do it. This book will help these people become millionaires as well; they may have to work just a little harder to make up for lost time.

Finally, career counselors who provide advice on jobs, careers, and professions will benefit from this book. It will provide them with a plan they can give to their clients to get them started down the right path.

Who is this book NOT for?

It is not for people who have no income. If you do not have a regular source of income, then you do not have the fundamental ingredient to start building wealth. It is not for people who insist they must spend every dime they earn. If your lifestyle requires more and more of everything you see, then you will never collect the necessary seed money to begin building your wealth. This book is also not for people who simply have no financial goals. Many people are perfectly happy living week to week and have no plans for the future. They have no worries about what will happen tomorrow. These people are enjoying their lives and should continue doing so for as long as they can.

This book is for people who are thinking long term, people who are preparing for their needs next year, next decade, and next career. In modern society, we have learned the difference between "have" and "have not". We may have become spoiled by becoming a "have". Life is good as a "have" and few people get excited about going back to being a "have not". If you are working on your future, building your education, improving your value to society and saving your money to create a better future for yourself and your family, then you are the perfect audience for this book.

Welcome to the Millionaire Employee Club. We are all working toward a similar long-term goal. We do not just want to be successful at work and make lots of money for the company, we also want to be successful for ourselves and make lots of money for our own futures.

Chapter 1

The Millionaire Investment Plan

Let's start with the assumption that everyone wants to be successful in his or her career and life. If this is not true about you, then you can stop reading right now and return this book to the store for a refund. If you are happy right where you are and want to stay there, then the plan that we describe in this book will not help you. In fact, it will fill your head with ideas about how to get ahead financially and probably confuse you and make you anxious about the "stay in place" plan that you have for your life.

Success is not just about money. There are many flavors of success that have nothing to do with money. But in modern society money has become a tool for accomplishing many of the things that we all want to do. If you want to feed your family, you can grow a garden. If you want to feed the world, you need a lot more resources—resources that are accessible through money.

This book begins with the plan that we laid out in *Becoming the Millionaire Employee*, and then digs deeper into the area of investing. If you follow the

Millionaire Employee plan, you will begin to accumulate money. But once you have that money, how will you put it to work? Will your money work as hard as you do? How will your money get its own job and create a stream of income—just like you do when you go to work every day? Your money cannot be a lazy bum that does no work and expects you to care and feed it constantly. Your money has to go to work every day. It has to earn a living. It has to bring home more bacon and not just sit in the bank and wait for you to give it the bacon.

Your Investing Plan

Do you have a plan for investing your money to enable it to grow for the rest of your life? Most people do not.

Most people do not even have a plan for saving money, much less investing it so that it grows.

People who have a plan for saving often stop there. They keep their money in a safe place. They keep their money in a mattress or a bank where they will not lose a penny, but where they also cannot make a dime.

If you have learned to save money, you have taken a big step toward becoming a millionaire employee. But you are not there yet. You need to take the next step and create a plan for investing that money.

People who are afraid to invest are focused on the pennies that they could lose, but have no understanding of the dollars they could make. You have to risk the pennies to make the dollars. Your money will not do anything on its own while locked in a bank vault.

If money was a rabbit, we could lock it in a cage and come back in a few months to find that it had multiplied. If you have two rabbits today, you could have twelve in just 30 days. These twelve could quickly multiply into 100, which could quickly become 1,000. All you have to do is feed the rabbits and keep them in the same pen together. If money was a rabbit, we would all be millionaires in just a few years. We could save two dollars, put it in a bank vault, and check it monthly to see how much it had multiplied. You would never have to put in more than two dollars because the money-rabbits would breed so quickly that putting more money into the vault would be like throwing another grain of sand on the beach—it would just get lost amid the millions of grains of sand.

Unfortunately, money in a bank vault does not behave like a pair of rabbits—it is more like a pair of turtles that never seem to get together. You have two of them this year and you will still have two next year. Banks let you deposit your money in their vaults. They even give you interest on that money. If you put $2 in the bank, you will not have $12 in one month the way you would if it was a money-rabbit. Instead, at 1% interest on bank deposits, your $2 will take 41 years to become $3. These are not money-rabbits. These are turtle-dollars. In fact, turtles move faster than that. You can make more money raising and selling turtles than you can by putting your money into a savings account. If you spend that $2 on a pair of breeding turtles, you will have a batch of baby turtles that you can sell in just nine or ten weeks. If you sell the entire batch for $1, then in less than three months you would have earned the same return that you would get in 41 years by keeping your $2.00 in a savings account.

Turtle-dollars should not discourage you from saving your money. It should just convince you that keeping your money in a bank savings account will not make you wealthy while you are still alive. Saving is just the first step in the millionaire plan. Next, you have to move on to investing your money.

If you already have a plan for becoming wealthy, it should be something you can write down for others to see. Your plan should be crystal clear in your mind. If you have a plan, write it down in the box below so you can see it yourself and keep track of how well you are following it.

My Current Investment Plan

1. _____

2. _____

3. _____

4. _____

5. _____

6. _____

As you look at this plan, ask yourself: *"Is this a millionaire plan? Will this plan reach a million dollars during my working life?"*

If the answers to these questions are *"Yes,"* you are in great shape. You have already worked out a plan for your financial future and you are following it. This book can give you some ideas to accelerate your plan. But the important thing is that you already have a millionaire plan in place.

If your answers to both questions are *"No,"* then you need this book. It will give you a plan that you can write down. This book will get you started down the road that leads to *"Yes"* to these questions.

The Millionaire Employee Plan

A plan for becoming a millionaire while spending your life as an employee does exist. You do not have to win the lottery, inherit money from your rich aunt, rob a bank, or find a missing Picasso painting in your attic.

If you put your efforts into developing unique and valuable skills and then apply these in your profession, you will earn enough money to save and invest your way to a million dollars.

Rule 1: Learn

Aristotle said,

> *"The educated differ from the uneducated as much as the living from the dead."*

As far back as 300 B.C., Aristotle recognized how essential it was to be an educated person. Science, philosophy, business, and other fields were still very young but were already changing the way societies developed. Education in these valuable fields was also separating the practitioners from the common man, and was already giving these people a big leg-up over the uneducated. Aristotle could see the night-and-day, or the living-and-dead, difference between these two classes of people.

This may be very harsh truth, but it is a truth that you need to use to your advantage. If you are educated, then use it. It you are not, then stop fighting against it and get educated. Aristotle made this observation over 2000 years ago and the importance of education during those 2000 years has not decreased—it has only increased.

The first step in the millionaire plan is to get educated. This is different from "getting an education." The word "an" here suggests that you just want one type of education. In practice, I recommend five specific pieces in your education plan.

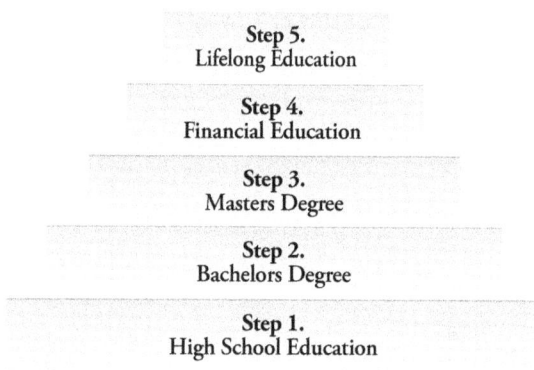

Step 5.
Lifelong Education

Step 4.
Financial Education

Step 3.
Masters Degree

Step 2.
Bachelors Degree

Step 1.
High School Education

Step 1: High School

The first step in getting an education is to finish high school. We are living in the 21st century, a time when there are almost no opportunities for success if you are a high school dropout. Even during your parent's generation, dropping out of high school meant a dead-end life. That is even truer today. In fact, you have to go back more than 100 years to reach a time in which dropping out of high school did not matter and a person could follow his or her dreams without this vital certificate of achievement.

Step 2: Bachelor's Degree

Once we entered the 20th century, most developed countries had moved beyond the knowledge learned in high school. Governments, companies, and other organizations were quickly becoming too complex to be mastered and controlled by high school level knowledge. The bachelor's degree was becoming the equivalent of the old high school diploma. This trend was visible before World War II and became even more obvious after that war in ended 1945.

In the 19th century, the ticket to success was the high school diploma. In the 20th century, it was the college bachelor's degree. Society does not move backward. It is always progressing. What was good enough yesterday will not be good enough tomorrow.

Step 3: Master's Degree

In the 21st century, a Master's Degree has become the ticket that lifts you above the masses of society and opens doors to opportunities that are unique, valuable, and rewarding. During the last two decades of the 20th century, a Master's Degree was rare for most business employees. Those who had one were often the leaders of their departments or corporations because they had acquired valuable knowledge that went beyond that of their peers who had a Bachelor's Degree. This was the time in which an MBA became all the rage for really getting ahead.

The proliferation of the MBA was just the beginning of this trend. In the 21st century, Master's Degrees are available and more common in almost all professionals. Some degrees focus on elite international investment bankers, while others are customized for the local bank loan officer. It is not unusual for the entering generation of engineers, managers, healthcare providers, and leaders in all industries to approach their very first job with a Master's Degree in hand. The younger generation sees the value of additional education and they are taking advantage of it while they are young, energetic, sharp, and unencumbered.

Step 4: Financial Education

Regardless of your professional field, you need to understand money, finances, and investments. As you work, you will accumulate extra money in the form of savings or retirement funds. You will find yourself holding thousands of dollars that are your responsibility to manage. This money can languish in a simple bank savings account for decades, unwatched and unchanged. But it will lose its purchasing power if you let it do that. The rate of inflation will be higher than your returns, effectively turning $100 into $99, then $98, then $97, then $90. If you do not take care of your money, it will not take care of you. It will whither and die like cut flowers in a vase. It will rust out like a car parked outside, exposed to the weather.

Accumulating money is both a blessing and a curse. You are blessed to have it. You are lucky to be in a profession that rewards you well enough to allow you to save. You are blessed with the security of having more than you need. You are also cursed with the need to learn to manage that money, to take care of it, to help it maintain its value, to enable it to support you when you really need it. Success brings responsibility. You cannot escape your own need to understand money and investing.

Step 5: Lifelong Education
The last step in your education is a continuous step. Learning is not just for the young. Learning is not something that you do until you are 18, or 22, or 25. Learning is a part of being human. As long as you are alive, you can and will be learning. Every day, you run into new people, have new experiences, and endure new challenges. You need to step up to each of these opportunities and grow. You need to learn how to do new things and solve new problems that you could not handle the day before.

Lifelong education might mean taking classes. It might mean reading books. It might mean jumping into new experiences. It might mean taking up new hobbies. It might mean listening to new ideas. Lifelong learning is what you choose to do every time you find something interesting or challenging in your life. You can choose to ignore everything new that you come across. Or you can choose to explore, learn, and conquer it. You can choose to become a master of many areas during your 80-, 90-, or 100-year life.

A life that spans a century cannot be based on education that was acquired by age 20. My grandmother was born in 1888. As a baby, she rode on her mother's lap in a covered wagon from Pennsylvania to Colorado. Her parents received a government land grant and moved west to become independent land owners and farmers. She grew up at the turn of the century, from the 19th to the 20th century. She was a married woman raising a family by the time World War I started. She lived in a farming community, raised eight children, and launched each of them into the world.

My grandmother was born just as the Industrial Revolution was transforming America into a world power. She lived to see the motorcycle and automobile completely replace the horse and covered wagon. She saw the birth of aviation. She watched the first rocket launches and lived to see men walk on the moon. The education she received from 1888 to 1908 was just the beginning of her understanding of the world and her ability to function in the 20th century.

If you were born in 1988 you are in your early 20s. You are facing the same worldwide changes that my grandmother saw. You may live to 2088 or beyond. You will see more changes in science, society, fashion, economy, and politics than my grandmother saw. The education you have today is not sufficient to carry you through your entire life until near the end of the 21st century. You need to be constantly learning. You need to grow and change along with the rest of society. You cannot afford to be outdated by the time you are 30 or 40. You will still have another 50 to 60 years ahead of you.

Lifelong education is a necessity and a privilege. It is more accessible and more valuable now than it has ever been. It is an essential part of your millionaire plan.

Rule 2: Earn

Before you can start saving money, you have to earn money. Graduating from college will open doors to good-paying jobs with nice benefits. This is where most millionaire employees get started and where most remain through their careers. You may change jobs a dozen or more times during your working life. You may take a chance and launch your own business. You may go back to school or on a missionary trip around the world.

In every case, you have to save money before you can invest it. And before you save money, you have to earn it. Before you earn it, you have to learn. Getting a job is just the beginning of the "Earn" rule. Thousands of professionals start a new job every year. Usually they are making a move up to a better position, higher pay, a better location, or a more significant opportunity.

When you are a college student looking for your first job, the jobs you come across look bigger and better than what you were doing to pay your expenses in college. When you are new to the job, it is not clear what is really expected of you. How do you do a good job, or a great job? How do you know when you are messing up this opportunity? How do you know when the axe is about to fall on your head?

If you want to maximize your earnings, you need to be aware of at least four basic practices while on the job.

First, just show up. Woody Allen said, *"Half the secret of success in life is just showing up."* Most people get a job and then get distracted by everything else that they want to do in life. They have a real problem showing up for work every day. They are not available when their boss or teammates need them. Just show up. This will put you above 50% of the people you work with.

Second, show up early. What is the difference between showing up at 8:00 AM and 8:30 AM? The difference is not 30 minutes; it is more like $3,000 a year. It is like moving your two-year promotion back to four years. Being late has a big impact on the company and your boss's perception of your value. Even though you may make up the time over lunch or at the end of the day, the damage has already been done. People have an image of you as a slacker because you arrive 10, 20, or 30 minutes after the expected time. With a little effort, you can be the person who shows up 10, 20, or 30 minutes before everyone else.

Third, work all of the time that you work. This seems like a novel concept, but you should be working when you are at work. That is why it is called "work" in the first place. If you are "at work" but spend your time chatting, cruising the halls, and getting lunch, then you are not actually working at work. Even some of the people who reliably show up for work forget to actually work once they are there. Everyone can tell the difference between the people who are working and the people who are just "at work".

Fourth, learn the mission of the company. Find out what is really important at your company. Every company is unique. You could spend your time on many different activities and many different projects. Find out which of these are the most important and spend your time and effort on them. How do you find out which are the most important? Ask the people who have been there for a few years. Ask for advice and guidance from the old hands. In addition to pointing you in the right direction, this will get people's attention. They will notice that you are actually interested in what is going on around the company and that you are actually interested in making a contribution where it counts the most. This is so rare that you will stand out.

These four top steps will help you earn the money that you will be investing. For a complete description of this plan, read *Becoming the Millionaire Employee*.

Rule 3: Spend

The first thing that most people do with the money they earn is spend it. They immediately convert income into outgo. Almost everything you do in life has a cost attached to it, and there has never been more to do than there is today. As a result, there are infinite ways to spend your money, and more services and products available than even the richest prince can afford. Even Bill Gates and Warren Buffet, the two richest men in the world, cannot afford to buy one of every product and every experience that exists. If they cannot afford it all, neither can you. You have to stop buying everything that catches your eye. You have to spend less than you earn.

Every millionaire spends less money than he or she earns. Without exception, the people who have money have gotten to where they are financially by not spending everything they earn.

America has become a nation of credit card addicts. We all have far too many credit cards and we use them ten times more often than we should. One of the key pieces of your millionaire spending plan is to pay as much toward your credit card balance as you charge to it during any given month. During the last month if you charged $500 to your credit card, the minimum payment that your credit card company will ask from you is about $40. Paying them $40 a month, plus 10%, 15%, or 20% in interest is the quickest way to go directly from having a decent paycheck to the poor house. You will dig yourself into a hole so deep that bankruptcy is the only way out of that hole.

Very few investments will return 10%, 15%, or 20% a year. You cannot get rich by putting $500 in an investment and carrying $500 in debt on your credit card. The net effect of this is negative income for you. Suppose your great investments return 10% and you have a 15% interest rate on your credit card. You will slide 5% further in debt each year despite having a great investment that returns 10%.

The second part of the spending plan is controlling how you spend your time and energy. You can use these essential resources to spend money or you can use them to acquire knowledge, skills, health, and relationships. If your major activity is shopping, then you are converting all the resources that make up your life into material possessions. You are turning your energy, time, and money into a new pair of pants or a new computer. At the end of the day and at the end of your life you will have lots of pants and lots of electronics but nothing else. You will not have used your life resources to purchase more health, more knowledge, or better relationships.

You only have enough time, energy, and money to acquire a limited amount of possessions, health, knowledge, and relationships. What balance of these do you want to have? Choose wisely because this is one of the most important decisions you will make about your life.

Rule 4: Save

The money you do not spend is available for saving: the first step toward investing. When you receive a paycheck, pay the most important person in the world first. This is the person who worked to bring in all of that money—you. Your efforts every month have earned you the right to be paid first. This does not mean paying bills you have racked up. It means putting the money into a piggy bank that will become your future wealth. It means growing your own personal assets faster than you contribute to the assets of the retailers in your neighborhood. You should benefit from the money you make more than your favorite clothing store does. They did not do anything to earn that money. They just put the clothes in a store, pushed advertisements on television, and waited for you to come in and give them all your money.

You have to pay yourself first every month. Pay yourself a fixed amount, or a growing amount. But do not skip or skimp for a month. Pay yourself fully every month.

There are two ways to start this pay-yourself-first plan. You can set a fixed amount right now and stick with that. Or you can start small and ratchet up the amount every month.

Fixed Amount

If you start with a fixed amount, then that amount should be at least 10% of your take home pay. That may sound like a lot, but it is the amount most likely to get you to a million dollars within 25 years. Anything less will take a lot longer. Many ancient religions considered a tithe to the church to be a 10% offering. They realized it was a realistic number for people to take out of their earnings. It was also substantial enough to enable the church to operate successfully. Saving 10% is strongly established throughout history and is supported by the mathematics of compounded returns on investments. It is the right number to start with.

1-2-3 Plan

If you have never saved money or if you already have very heavy bills, then you may find it impossible to start saving 10% immediately. In that case, an alternative that lets you tip-toe into the saving business might help. During the first month, save 1%, or a single penny out of every dollar you make. That is such a small amount that you probably lose this much in loose change every month. Create a 1% transfer from your checking to your savings account. Next month, increase that to 2%. The following month, increase your savings rate to 3%.

Each month, increase your savings rate by 1%. By the end of the year, you will be at 12%. Do not stop when you reach 10%. Since you started slowly, you need to make up for it by saving more than 10% for a while. When you reach 12% at the end of one year, think about continuing to push that number up by 1% every month. You might set a goal of reaching 15%, 20%, or 25%. These levels are not impossible, and many people save this amount every month and have done so for years. You are discovering the upper limit of how much you can really save.

Every month, pay yourself first, and pay yourself at least 10% of your take-home pay.

Rule 5: Invest

In *Becoming the Millionaire Employee*, I gave you an outline for investing the money you save. It is a very basic strategy that focuses on specific categories of investment vehicles. But it did not go into detail about these investments, which is the focus of this book. I first want to recap the investment advice from the first book.

First, you must take advantage of an individual retirement account (IRA) or a 401(K). Both of these vehicles allow you to save your money tax-free. The money you put in and the interest or returns that it attracts all grow without being taxed year-to-year. Taxes are assessed when you take the money out, most likely once you retire. This tax-free growth is like getting an additional 2% to 4% in returns every year. The money that is not taken out as taxes remains in the account and creates more growth. These accounts are such a good deal that they should be the first form of investment that you take advantage of. You can find more details on the IRA, the Roth IRA, and the 401(K) in *Becoming the Millionaire Employee* or in a number of other excellent investment books.

IRA and 401(K) accounts usually allow you to put your money into a number of different investments. You can choose mutual funds, stocks, bonds, or treasuries. Which are the best choices for you? That is one of the key questions that we answer in this book.

Second, you have to hang out with people with the same goals that you have—or with people who have already accomplished what you are shooting for. If you are trying to become a millionaire, you will not figure out everything that you need to know on your own. You need to be connected with other people who are trying to achieve the same goals. These people will find different information and opportunities than those you find. They need your knowledge and you need theirs. You will become like the people you hang out with. In a negative sense, *"bad company corrupts good character."* And, good company encourages good character. Arrange to work around, socialize with, and exchange ideas with people who are focused on becoming millionaires. Do not spend all of your time with people who only want to throw away their money, energy, and time.

Third, develop the mind of an investor. Investors see investments as powerful ways to apply their money. They see opportunity in investing more than in spending. They understand the difference between 10% of their salary spent at the mall and 10% placed in an investment. They are motivated to direct significant portions of their money into areas that will grow this money and make them better off tomorrow than they are today.

Fourth, initially you may not understand investments, risks and rates of return, but that is normal. Everyone starts off uneducated and confused about investments. Feel free to watch and learn. Although you can start saving immediately, you may need some time before you are ready to invest intelligently. Feel free to take the time to read, talk to others, and practice online. Investing is about a few basic ideas and principles that you need to master quickly once you start digging into the topic.

Fifth, buy stock not stuff. We all know which products we are eager to get our hands on. Some of us have a passion for computers, some for clothes, and others for dinners at restaurants. Each week, you make decisions about whether to spend more money on these products. But knowing where you and others are eager to spend your money is a good tip to where you might invest your money. Once a month, decide to buy the stock of a company instead of buying their stuff. If you have a family, you might easily spend $100 on a nice dinner for four at the Olive Garden. This same $100 buys you three shares of Darden Restaurant stock, the parent company of Olive Garden. A year from now, the meal that you would have had at the Olive Garden will be long gone and forgotten. But the three shares of Darden stock will still be in your portfolio. In a sense, that stock is free to you because you would have eaten it otherwise. Therefore, at any price, the stock has a higher value than the meal you skipped one year ago. Buy Stock, Not Stuff.

These are five great ways to get started with your investments. Have you tried all of these? If not, then it is time that you take action right now. Each of these steps is a start before you get into the details found in this second book.

Rule 6: Incorporate

The last rule for becoming a millionaire employee is to create your own corporation. Although in your day job, you are an employee of a larger organization; your success will require that you have the protection and the tax advantages that come with a corporate umbrella. Over time, you will have more and more assets that need to be handled as a business. When your money earns money, it becomes a business just like your employer's business. Eventually, your personal funds will grow larger than the amount you earn every year. You need to organize and protect this money in the same way that IBM and General Electric organize and protect their assets.

Dozens of different forms of incorporation exist. The one that you are most likely to call on first is the Limited Liability Corporation (LLC). The LLC allows you to hold assets in a corporation that is separate from your personal assets, but that is controlled and owned by the LLC's investors, which is primarily you. As a corporation, the LLC can balance investing expenses against its income, allowing you to deduct the costs that you encounter before being taxed on your earnings.

The LLC also provides legal protection if your investment company includes assets that might attract legal action. Direct ownership of real estate assets is one example. The LLC is a separate entity from your personal investments; therefore, legal action can be contained within the LLC, protecting your personal assets (or vice versa).

Many legal and tax details surround the advantages and operations of a corporation. Your state government maintains a "Department of Corporations" or something similar at which you will find details specific to your location. You can do the incorporation paperwork yourself and pay the fee to the state. But you might also want to read other books on this topic. You may also want to hire a lawyer or accountant to help you get some of the details right.

Millionaire Employee Investor

The six rules of the millionaire employee are clear, basic, and essential. You cannot become a millionaire as an employee if you do not follow these rules. Millions of people have the potential to become millionaires over their lifetime, but they do not take advantage of it. For these people their life's energy, time, and money flow through their hands and into the waiting hands of others who are more serious about becoming wealthy.

If you are to get serious about becoming a millionaire you will follow the six big rules that are outlined here and described in more detail in *Becoming the Millionaire Employee*. These will lead you to accumulating the money that needs to be invested. How and where should it be invested? That is what this book is all about.

Chapter 2

The Piggy Bank

A s children, many of us received a piggy bank as a gift from our parents or a relative. The image of the pig is a cute way of getting a child's attention and building an interest in the idea of saving pennies, nickels, dimes, and quarters. The piggy bank might introduce children to the very idea of deciding to save money instead of spending it. Little kids can accept the idea that the money is still within reach, as they can save it today, but spend it tomorrow if they want to. Putting a dime into the back of the pig is a very small commitment when you know you can pull the cork out of the belly and get that dime back any time you want.

Why is this little bank shaped like a pig? Those from farming communities assume that it is just a common animal around the farm. In fact, the source of the term and the shape is much older than that notion. Nearly 1,000 years ago, the word "pygg" meant a specific type of clay used to make household pottery, including jars. These pygg jars stored oils, liquids, and grains, and were basic containers for everyday life. Everything was stored in a pygg jar, including money. Eventually, the pygg jar that contained money came to be referred to as the pygg bank. So, a big bank was a key business in the community, and a pygg bank held all of the money in the home.

Some time during the 18th century, the spelling of pygg clay was changed to "pig" and the pygg bank became the pig bank. Once that happened, creating jars shaped like a pig which were also made from pygg clay was just a tiny step away. Then, as glass, plaster, and plastic materials were introduced, they naturally replaced pygg clay, but the pig bank retained its shape regardless of its material.

That is the origin of the Western piggy bank. Slotted money boxes were invented all over the world in ancient times. There are clay temples with money slots in the top dating from 200BC. Though these are not strictly piggy banks, they certainly attempted to help people save their coins in a vessel where it could not be easily extracted.

When my little brother turned five years old, my older cousin Margene made a ceramic pig for him in a crafts class. It had the classic pig shape and its sides were painted with ribbons and gems. It had the classic money slot at the top and a corked hole at the bottom. Both he and I spent our childhood putting our dimes in the top during the week and taking them out of the bottom over the weekend. The little pig was nothing more than a pretty bowl in which we stored our coins until it was time to use them.

The piggy bank was more like a checking account for children than a savings account.

Recognizing that the cork in the bottom was a fundamental weakness in the piggy bank's ability to teach savings, some manufacturers eliminate the cork hole. The only way in or out of the pig was through the small slot in the top. This meant that making a withdrawal was a major event. It required smashing the ceramic pig to access the coins. But children are clever little creatures. Since they are motivated to get those dimes out of the pig, most of them quickly learned that turning the pig upside down, inserting a knife into the slot, and shaking the pig could line up the dimes and have them fall out into our eager little hands. Even without the withdrawal hole in the bottom, the pig remained a checking account instead of a savings account.

This characteristic of pulling money out of any form of banking device and spending it is not unique to children. Adults break into their life's savings all the time to pay for the luxuries they just cannot do without. Adults pull the cork out of the bottom or slide the butter knife into the top of their savings, just like little children. Their thinking about money and their respect for saving has not developed much since they were five years old.

Money in the Mattress

People who do not trust banks go to great lengths to find a way to keep their money in a safe place. Once you have too much money to fit into a piggy bank, where do you keep it? Maybe you hide it under, or inside, a mattress. Maybe you bury it in the ground where no one will look for it. Both of these have a long history as a form of savings.

When money cannot be trusted to a banker because he might be crooked or the bank might be robbed, where can it go? If you are a Greek or Roman peasant, you have only a few personal possessions. You might own a couple of dishes for eating, a few farming implements, and a bed of straw to sleep on. The most secure of all of these items is the bed. Perhaps a few coins mixed in with the straw will go unnoticed by a thief who raids your home while you are working in the field. Although a very weak form of security, for an impoverished peasant it is about the only option available for saving the small sums needed to buy food during the week.

Once the money becomes more plentiful, it can no longer be hidden in the mattress. It has to be put into a larger vault. If you cannot purchase a building with a vault, then the good mother Earth will have to be your vault. Your key to that vault is a secret location and a shovel. You wrap your money in a cloth or put it into a pygg jar and slip off to a hidden location. With your shovel, you unlock your personal safe deposit box in the ground, insert the money, and lock it tight by shoveling the dirt back over it. Your life savings are now safely locked up and only someone with the two keys can get to it. The first key is its location and the second is a shovel.

By legend, this earthen safe deposit box was the banking system of the Caribbean pirates. They were said to have roamed the seas looking for merchant ships to attack and rob. In the movies, these merchants carried chests full of gold, silver, and gems. There seemed to be more gold floating about than any of us has seen in a lifetime. Even the entire contents of a large modern jewelry store could barely fill one of the chests that the pirates steal during their raids. Once the treasure was claimed, the pirates ran off to a remote and uncharted island to bury it in the sand. Supposedly, none of the sailors wanted their treasure at that moment, but preferred that the captain keep it for them in a hole in the ground for a few months or years. Once back in port, the pirates wanted nothing more than to sleep in a clean bed and walk the streets. They had no use for treasure that would require them to buy food, clothing, liquor, and company.

In truth, burying treasure was rare for real pirates. The goods they took from merchant ships were more in the form of ships riggings, medicine, clothing, food, and tools. All of these were needed simply to survive and none of the crew had any other form of income with which to purchase them. Any form of money, especially gold and silver, was divided between the captain, the officers, and the crew according to a specific formula in which the captain received two to ten times as much as an ordinary seaman.

What kept the pirates working was the hope for at least one big haul during their entire lives. This would allow them to retire and live in luxury any place they chose, assuming they were not caught by the authorities or robbed by other pirates. This once-in-a-lifetime strike was often recorded to be around £1,000 for a common seaman and many times this for the captain. But £1,000 during the 17th century was equivalent to over a million dollars today. In fact, Captain Thomas Tew seized an Indian merchant ship in 1692 that was so loaded with gold that each sailor received £3,000, or nearly $3.5 million. Tew himself received £7,500 or nearly $10 million.

The pirating business was essentially the dot-com startup of its age. Pirates made one raid after another, but if they could just have one successful venture in their lifetime it would pay off more than they could earn from a lifetime of employment in any other field.

Burglars

Putting your money into a piggy bank or a mattress, or burying it in the ground may seem safe and secure, but these are the worst ways to save and invest your money. All are exposed to two major thieves. The first—and worst of these—is you. Typically, the owner of these investments just cannot keep his or her hands out of the cookie jar. The money is too close by. It is too accessible. It is too idle. All of us find good reason to break out the butter knife or the shovel to retrieve the money we are supposed to be saving. The temptation of everyday spending is just too great to resist day after day after day. Every day, you find new reason to rob yourself of your savings and go shopping. Every day, you have a new bill that you can take care of easily by digging into the piggy bank.

Many people who invest by hiding their money fear that a burglar will break in and rob them of all of their hard earned cash. That is possible, but remote. The mysterious burglar is much less common that the ever-present owner of the money who has other ways to spend it. We rob ourselves much more frequently than we are robbed by strangers.

No Interest Earned in the Mattress

Finally, your money in a piggy bank or a hole in the ground earns no interest. The money is completely idle and is not working for you. It is not earning its keep. When you put $100 in a mattress, it will remain $100 in a mattress. It will never grow to $101.

Most of us do not earn enough money to save our way to one million dollars. We all rely on long-term investment returns. We all rely on our money to have just a little bit of a rabbit in it. We turn $100 that we save into $500 through the returns we earn over the years. In fact, if you were to invest just $10,000 in something that could earn a 10% return, in 50 years you would have over $1 million. Your money would multiply itself by 100 while invested. But if you put that same $10,000 into a hole in the ground and dug it up 50 years later, it would still be $10,000.

Even worse, the $10,000 in the ground will not have the same buying power in 50 years as it did when you buried it. All modern societies operate with some degree of inflation. With an average inflation rate of 3% over those 50 years, it would take nearly $45,000 to buy the same package of goods that you could get for $10,000 when you buried the money. At this rate, that $10,000 is only worth about $2,222 after 50 years.

So, using a piggy bank or a hole in the ground to invest is not a way to stay even. Even if you are the strongest willed saver on the planet and can keep yourself from dipping into these savings, the money will deteriorate as it sits there. Inflation is a burglar who breaks into your house every year and steals just 3% of what is in your piggy bank. It is the pirate who digs up your buried treasure and steals just 3% at a time, leaving the remaining 97%, hoping you will not notice what is missing.

People who hide their money usually do not notice that 3% disappears every year. Their understanding of money and the economy is so weak that $100 in the pig looks like it is still worth $100 every year. They are deceived or misinformed. They are going broke and do not even know it is happening.

Putting $100 into the piggy bank or the hole in the ground is better than not saving anything at all, but not by much. Learning to hold onto money is a necessary first step toward learning about investing it. But it is far from the last step you need to take. It is the beginning of a long, exciting, and rewarding journey of adventure and discovery.

If you have $100 or $1000 in a piggy bank, get ready to move it. But don't get ready to spend it.

Chapter 3

The Big Bank

Eventually, people who store their money in a pygg jar or a hole in the ground cannot sleep at night. They have so much money stashed away that they are plagued by a fear that someone will discover it and take it away from them. People need a place to put their money that will put their minds at ease, a place that will let them sleep at night. But who can you really trust with your precious pile of cash?

Rich land owners might construct a castle, and within that castle build a vault guarded by soldiers who are guarded by more soldiers. This is a very expensive way to hold money. It is the "Fort Knox" solution of valuing and protecting items like gold, jewels, coins, and eventually paper money. These vaults become something of great interest to other barons, kings, and, armies. They are a potential source of quick wealth. If you can just raise an army large enough to breach the walls of the castle, kill all the guards, and then burst into the vault, you can become a richer king or baron. And, once you have such an army what do you do with them after you sack the first castle? Since they are so good at this job, you are now in the business or sacking cities, robbing barons, and pillaging entire countries. This is the story of many ancient wars, feuds, and crusades. The entire war started as a single bank robbery that just got out of hand.

Surely there must be a better way to store valuables than putting them in a big vault inside a castle. Who really wants the gold anyway? You can't do a whole lot with gold, silver, and jewels. They are pretty, but you can't build a home with them, weave them into clothing, eat them for dinner, or ride them down the road. What you really want is the ability to use the wealth to get what you want, but without the worries and responsibilities of storing it. Wouldn't it be much better if you just had a book or scrap of paper that said that you had so much gold in a vault that could never be robbed? The paper is easy to store or carry. It is easy to show to other people. It might be possible to give other people a small share of your paper receipt in exchange for some clothing or food.

This was the evolution of paper money. It was a way to deliver a receipt for gold on deposit somewhere safe. Paper money is so much more convenient than heavy and difficult-to-divide gold and jewels. Before long, every modern country shifted to the receipt-based form of exchange.

In the beginning, each paper bill was directly exchangeable for a certain amount of gold. People had a hard time accepting that a piece of paper was as valuable as a piece of gold. Even though neither could be turned directly into food or clothing, gold was considered more solid and dependable. But in 1971 President Nixon eliminated the "gold standard" and finally shifted the country to a system of money based on its productivity and net worth.

Having money in paper form was the beginning of the creation of a receipt-based exchange mechanism. These receipts may be easier to carry, but they are still valuable and need to be protected. How do you hold onto a lot of receipts when you do not need them immediately?

Well, you need to be able to rent a vault. Or even better, find someone else who needs the receipts right now and is willing to pay you to hold onto them. In exchange for your dollar (one form of receipt), this person will give you another receipt that says that they owe you money. In addition, they will pay you a small fee to use the money while they have it. This person has a need for the money now and will pay you to use your money for a while.

This is the function of a bank. A bank is a business developed specifically to provide a trusted place to store money while you are not using it.

Banks actually began as moneychangers. They had enough money to provide lending services to others who needed that money immediately. In exchange for a fee, these moneychangers allowed you to use their money for certain period. There is evidence that moneylenders existed back to 350 B.C. A coin from the city of Trapezus in ancient Rome shows the table of a moneylender stacked high with coins. These lenders were the origin of the banks. They typically set up their tables in city squares, like any other vendor. Customers visited them when they visited the butcher, baker, or clothing maker during a typical visit to the city—very similar to shopping today.

The moneylenders' bench was called a "bancu." Over time, covering the bancu in a green cloth to identify it as a place to exchange money became a common practice. The Italian word "bancu" became the modern term "bank." The green tablecloth became the green color of paper bills, the green visor of the banker/accountant, and the universal color to represent money and wealth.

In 1407, the first state deposit bank was established in Genoa, Italy. This is the same city that gave the world Christopher Columbus later in the same century. The Banco di San Giorgio allowed certain citizens to create accounts to store their wealth and made that wealth available as loans to help others to conduct and grow their businesses.

Moneylenders and banks became essential players in the growth of cities and nations. Storing money safely was a very minor part of their value to society. Much larger was the service they provided in putting the wealth of the city to work by lending it out. They turned hoarded piles of gold, cash, and valuables into working capital that improved entire cities and populations. In creating so much value for society, they also created a healthy source of income for the banker, which has always been resented by those who performed other kinds of labor.

If you are part of a society that does not trust banks, then you are carrying on a mental tradition from over 2,000 years ago. This distrust has been reinforced in every country about every 50 years. Your parents or grandparent may have been burned if they lost money in a bank during the Great Depression. Millions of people lost billions of dollars during that period. The Great Depression was so difficult on the entire country that the U.S. government and its banking system realized they could not allow the hard-earned wealth of every citizen to be at risk in an unregulated banking system. Therefore, the government created an insurance system to reimburse every depositor for the funds they may lose. Like all insurance policies, this policy—the Federal Deposit Insurance Corporation (FDIC)—spreads the risks and the payments for failure across the entire population. Today, you can rest assured that your money in an FDIC insured bank will not be lost as a result of a bank failure or illegal activities. These banks are allowed to offer a number of regulated products, some which can lose money, but the risks of each of these products must be disclosed to the person buying them.

Banking is too essential to the health of an entire nation and the economic activity of the entire world to be allowed to operate without regulation and without protecting the individuals and corporations who use such services.

When you put your money in a bank, you are doing two things. First, you entrust it to one of the largest and safest vaults that you can find. You put your money in a place from which it cannot be lost or stolen. Given the role of the FDIC, this money cannot be stolen from you. A modern bank robber may walk into the bank and take every single bill and coin in the building. But the coins that he takes are not the ones you deposited. The stolen money comes out of the pockets of the larger banking system and the government, not out of the pockets or accounts of the individual depositors. This insurance and assurance makes a bank a perfect safe haven for your money.

Second, you are taking that step of allowing your money to earn more money. You begin to understand that the money you save is valuable to you, and has value to other people. Because other people need it, you can charge them a fee to use your money. You can deposit $100 or $1000 in the bank and earn interest on it because the bank is lending that money to other people, and you get to share the interest they charge for lending it out. Since the bank is doing all of the work and assuming all of the risk involved, they also keep a larger share of the interest they make from lending out your money. Your share is smaller because you are a passive participant and because the bank is providing you with a safe place to keep your money. And, they provide that service essentially for free.

When you are ready to move from your piggy bank to the local bank on the corner, the bank can offer you three major money management products: a checking account, a savings account, and certificates of deposit. These products are great ways for you to become familiar and comfortable with saving and investing your money. They are a great start and are very safe. But they are far from the last options that you have.

In truth, a bank does not exist because you need a safe place to save your money. It exists because others need a place from which they can borrow money. Most banks accumulate the money they lend out by accepting deposits like yours. But they make their money through their lending activities. If a bank offers nothing more than a safe place to store your wealth, then they would have to charge you a fee for that service. When they can also lend the money to others and earn interest on those funds, they can offer you free deposit services and, in fact, pay you to keep your money there.

This is essentially why you pay for a safe deposit box at your bank, as whatever you put into the safe deposit box is "dead money." The bank cannot use it to help other people. Those funds cannot pay for new buildings or businesses. So you have to pay someone to keep it safe for you. Those valuables sit quietly in a dark box doing nothing at all. Their value is simply in remaining safe and unchanged for years, decades, or centuries.

Bank Accounts

As a future investor, one of the best concepts you learn from your bank accounts is the trusting of others with your money, as well as the practice of reading the fine print on the conditions under which banks serve you. You will also learn to understand the concepts of interest and compound rates of return.

Banking is "Investing 101." It is something that everyone in a modern society has to learn. Even the most uneducated and least ambitious people in society have to know how to use a bank to save, borrow, and earn.

Interest Rates

The first concept that is usually new to people is the interest rate or rate of return on the money they put into an account, or that they take out as a loan. The interest rate is the fundamental factor that makes banking work. It is the only reason that your neighborhood bank exists. Your bank earns interest from loans it makes and sometimes from the services it provides. The bank also pays interest to people who deposit money with them. They do this to attract more money that they can use to make more loans.

It is possible for a local bank to be formed with just investments from a few wealthy people. The money these people deposit makes them founders and owners. It can also allow them to start lending their own money and earning interest. Nearly all the interest they earn from these loans can go directly back to them. They just have to give up a little of this return to cover the operating expenses of their bank. Such a bank might operate for years based just on the personal funds of a few people who started it. But eventually, this bank will reach the limit set by federal and state governments on the number of dollars that they are allowed to lend based on how much the owners put in. To grow, they need to attract more money. Most neighborhood banks do this by opening themselves up to deposits from local citizens and businesses and offer to pass on a share of the interest they earn to such people or businesses.

Some banks are open to all depositors; others limit themselves to accepting money from specific businesses, professionals, or localities. These details are important to the bankers and bank owners, but are not very relevant to depositors. Depositors just want to know their money is safe, as in insured by the FDIC, and what interest rate they will receive.

Interest is offered in two basic forms: simple and compound. Simple interest gets its name from being the simplest idea there is to earning interest. If you deposit $100 at a simple interest rate of 5%, then at the end of one year you receive $5 in interest, along with your original deposit of $100.

Next year you can do the same with the whole $105. Or you can spend your $5 interest payment and just keep the $100 in the bank, or any number of variations on this and it is easy to understand. If you leave the entire $105 in the bank for a second year, then you will earn 5% interest on that money. At the end of the second year, you will have earned $5.25 in interest and have a total balance of $110.25. You earned an additional 25 cents in the second year because you started with a slightly higher amount by leaving the $5 from the first year in your account. If you leave all of your money in the bank for a third year, then you begin with a balance of $110.25, which will earn 5%. At the end of that year, the bank will give you the interest you earned, about $5.51 and your account balance will be $115.76.

This is called simple interest because there is just one calculation done each year.

Compound interest is a little more complex, but not much more. If the bank offers you that same 5% interest rate, but "compounded quarterly," then they are making a little more complex calculation for how much they will pay you. The bank is calculating your interest using the same rate, but they are depositing the interest in your account at the end of each quarter, or every three months. You do not earn 5% in three months. Instead, you earn one quarter of this every three months, and this amount is added to your account at that time. So, that same $100 in an account that earns 5% interest compounded quarterly grows a little every quarter (every three months) instead of just once a year. Does that really make a difference?

Your initial deposit earns one quarter of 5% after the first quarter. So you get 5% divided by 4, or 1.25%, added to your account. At the end of the first three months, you have $101.25 in your account. When you let that ride into the second quarter, you earn 1.25% interest on $101.25, not just the $100 you started with. During the second quarter, the interest you earn will be:

$$\$101.25 * (5\%/4) = \$1.265625, \text{ or about } \$1.27$$

This money is added to your account and at the end of the second quarter you will have $102.52. If you do this for four quarters, you will have earned $5.10 in interest at the end of one year and will have a total balance of

$105.10 in your account. Your money grows a little faster with compounding because you earn interest on your past interest each quarter instead of just once a year. In just one year, this is equivalent to depositing your money in an account that earns 5.1% in simple interest. If you let this money grow over many years, the rate of growth actually increases each year, just as you saw it increase each quarter in this example.

Over time, the banking industry has come to describe their interest rates as either:

**5% simple interest, or
5% compounded quarterly.**

There is nothing special about compounding every quarter. A bank can offer interest compounded monthly, weekly, daily, hourly, or even continuously. The math to keep track of each of these is almost the same as in the example above. It just has to be done more frequently. Before the use of computers, the frequency of compounding was limited by how many people that a bank wanted to hire to calculate these numbers and write them down in paper ledgers. That is the real reason quarterly interest became so prevalent. Today, we have millions of large and small computers doing this work and automatically storing the results in databases. The only reason people do this work by hand today is to learn the concept behind the calculation. Once they get the idea down, they then let the computers do the calculations.

Another advantage of computers is that you do not have to round off the fractional pennies as I did in the example. In the second quarter above, the interest earned was actually $1.265625, which I rounded to $1.27 for brevity. A computer accurately calculates the numbers rather than rounding up that last half penny.

How much can $100 grow to at 5%, without any additional deposits from you? The following table shows this money growing at both 5% simple interest and 5% compounded quarterly for 20 years.

Table 3-1. 5% Interest Over 20 Years

Year	5% Simple Interest	5% Compounded Quarterly
0	$100.00	$100.00
1	$105.00	$105.09
2	$110.25	$110.45
3	$115.76	$116.08
4	$121.55	$121.99
5	$127.63	$128.20
6	$134.01	$134.74
7	$140.71	$141.60
8	$147.75	$148.81
9	$155.13	$156.39
10	$162.89	$164.36
11	$171.03	$172.74
12	$179.59	$181.54
13	$188.56	$190.78
14	$197.99	$200.50
15	$207.89	$210.72
16	$218.29	$221.45
17	$229.20	$232.74
18	$240.66	$244.59
19	$252.70	$257.05
20	$265.33	$270.15

You can see that over 20 years the effect of compounding can earn you an additional $4.82. This is your second lesson in interest rates. They grow your money at different rates depending on how they are applied.

Checking Accounts

Banks offer checking accounts for the convenience of the customer. The bank cannot do a whole lot with the money that you put in this account. Since your money comes in every week or month from your paycheck, it is usually withdrawn by the end of the month to pay bills. This money moves through checking accounts too quickly for the bank to lend it to other customers. As a result, most banks do not pay an interest rate on checking account balances. In fact, most banks charge a fee for you to have a checking account. Checking is a service that benefits you but is difficult for banks to make a profit from.

Most people use their checking account as a conduit between the money they earn and the money they spend. Their checks go into the account and their bills get paid. Your checking account should also be a conduit to your investing accounts. Just as you make regular payments for your mortgage, your electricity bill, and your car, you should make regular payments to your investing accounts. Your investing should be at least as important as your spending.

It is easy to determine whether spending or investing is more important to you. If you watch your money moving through your checking account, do you allow your bills to grow so large that you occasionally have to skip making a payment into your investing accounts? If you do, then that is a sure sign that consumption and spending control you more than investing does.

Your checking account pays your debts every month. But the largest debt you have is to yourself. It is your obligation to take care of your own and your family's financial future. You do this by saving and investing. Each month, your checking account should pay the most important person first—you.

You have to take care of your own future needs just as regularly as you take care of your current bills. Most people find this hard to do. No matter how much money they make, they ratchet up their spending to a point where every penny they make is spent on current consumption. The result is that their ability to save and invest is not dependent on how much they make but on how much they spend. You have to stop spending as much as you make. You have to dial it back so you can save at least 10% of the money you make.

Your checking account plays a central role in how you distribute your money. This is where your earning, spending, saving, and investing activities meet. It is where you compare your bills, credit cards, and daily expenses with how much money you make. In other words, how your money flows through your checking account tells you a great deal about your financial future. If you constantly drain your checking account before you reach the end of each month and before you have a chance to move money into your savings and investment accounts, then you are spending too much and you will be in trouble. If you are able to move money from your checking into your savings and investing accounts, then you have a potentially great future ahead.

It is your financial, moral, and social responsibility to control your own spending. No one else will do this for you. As explained in *Becoming the Millionaire Employee*, thousands of businesses reach out to you every day to make you spend every penny you earn. All they want is for you to give everything you earn and more to them in the form of purchases. You have to ignore them and learn to control your spending. Do not let them control you. They will ruin you if you do.

Savings Accounts

A savings account allows you to accumulate money, earn interest, and keep it liquid enough to enable you to get to it when you need it. The purpose of a savings account is usually to build up enough money for a specific need in the future. This may be a down payment for a house or a car or to cover tuition in a few years. It may be to start a business or it may be an emergency fund that you will use if something terrible happens, like losing your job or incurring medical expenses.

The key feature of a bank savings account is that it is liquid, which means you can get your money out almost immediately if you need to. The bank understands this money will usually reside with them longer than it will in a checking account. In fact, many banks are built on the money accumulated in savings accounts, as these are funds the bank can lend to others. Because such funds can be put to use profitably by banks, most banks share a portion of the interest they earn with you. A savings account carries a small interest rate, less than what the bank makes on loans because your interest is a fraction of that loan interest.

You should automatically transfer some portion of your income from your checking to your savings account every month. With a savings account, you will learn about accumulating money over longer periods and you will see the compounding effect of a low interest rate. In the world of investing, a savings account offers one of the lowest interest rates available. These rates are low because the risk to you is low. In America, the risk of losing money in a savings account is almost zero. A savings account is a sure thing. But with little risk comes little reward. You cannot earn great returns from a savings account.

Eventually, you will outgrow your savings account. You will find that it has enough money to make the payment you had anticipated or serves well as an emergency fund. Where do you go from there? Your local bank has one more product to offer.

Certificates of Deposit

A certificate of deposit (CD) is similar to a savings account, but with a contract attached. You agree to place a specified amount into a CD and to leave it with the bank for a specific period. CD contracts are typically three months, six months, or one year. In exchange for agreeing to lock up your money for a few months, the bank gives you a higher interest rate. Because you will not take out any of this money during the period of the contract, the bank can use this money more aggressively. It can invest it such that it earns a higher rate of return, and can afford to share a little more of that return with you than they can from the amount they make on money in a savings account.

CDs are also insured by the federal government and represent an almost no-risk investment option. You can get a higher rate on a CD because of what the bank can do with the money, but your return is still limited by the low risk that you take with it. If a savings account pays 1%, then a CD might pay as much as 3%. The rate also increases as the length of time that you agree to leave money in the CD increases.

Conduit to Bigger Investing

Many banks attempt to offer more advanced investment services. They may serve as a broker to buy and sell stocks and bonds. They make an attempt to meet all of your financial needs. But this convenience comes with a price, as their fees are usually a little higher than that of other companies. Also, their focus on local branches means they cannot offer the level of expertise that you need for more advanced investments. The staff members at local bank branches are not investors or investment managers. You need to find this expertise elsewhere.

I also prefer to separate my banking from my investing to create a clear distinction between the money that I use for my regular needs and the money that I set aside to grow into future wealth. Holding my investment money an additional step away from the money I spend helps remind me not to pull investing money backward to meet my short-term needs.

As we said before, the local bank is a great place to get started and it offers a few accounts that can be very useful to you. More importantly, it is a conduit from the daily churn of your money through a checking account into deeper pools of saving and investing. Your local bank is the first stop in diverting money from your daily or monthly earnings into your long-term wealth.

Once your checking and savings accounts are operating smoothly, it is time to move on to more advanced forms of investing.

Chapter 4

The Wide World of Investing

Walk into a large department or discount store and begin counting the number of different products on the shelves. Or just limit yourself to one section of the store and count the number of brands and variations of shampoo, conditioner, and hair spray. Walk through the sporting goods section and try to count all of the different pieces of equipment and accessories. You will begin to get an idea of how many millions of different products exist. You could count over 100 different shampoos and conditioners, or several hundred pieces of sports equipment. A single large store could have over 100,000 unique items for sale.

The world and our country have become very productive and very competitive. Manufacturers try to create unique products even though many of them are almost identical to those that exist. But a uniquely shaped bottle, a new label color, a new "silkiness" to the shampoo, a catchy marketing angle, or a well-know spokesperson can attract millions of customers and make a sensation from a product that is identical to hundreds of others already available.

The world of investing is part of this huge proliferation and marketing of unique products. Thousands of different investment products are available, as are hundreds of minute variations on each truly unique product. A new shopper for an investment can be overwhelmed with all of the choices. It is like wandering into a giant department store for the very first time and seeing an ocean of products that you never imagined could exist.

When the Iron Curtain that separated the Western world from the Soviet Republic fell, thousands of people were able to leave their country for the first time and see what other places were like. Many of these people were particularly mesmerized by the American grocery store. For the first time, they walked into a building that had more food in it than anyone could purchase. They saw hundreds of types of bread, cheese, meat, vegetables, and fruit. These former Soviet citizens could not believe that such a place could be real. Many thought that it must be political propaganda. They had no idea that such abundance could exist or that an average citizen could be wealthy enough to shop in such a store. Their amazement, bewilderment, and inability to understand everything they were looking at is very similar to the experience of a new investor trying to sort through all the investment products offered.

Most people face this confusion when they get started. Each is at the mercy of the investment advisory or advertisement that catches his or her attention. A new investor may wander into a company or a product that is not at all appropriate for him or her, but just happens to catch him or her in its clutches.

This chapter provides some order to the confusion of advertisements and products. Although hundreds of different ways to invest may exist, there are a few major categories of investments. Some are not at all appropriate for a new investor or for an investor who has a full-time job and is trying to manage his or her money on the side.

Always remember that some people do nothing except invest and many products are targeted just at that type of person. Others are already rich and are interested only in minimizing the taxes they pay each year. Some are retired and have a nest egg they want to live off for the rest of their lives. Unique products have been created for these people and those in many other situations. These products are probably not right for you.

This chapter briefly reviews several investment vehicles that are appropriate for young professionals just getting started. Such people are working hard at their jobs, saving their money, and looking to put that money to work until it turns into a million dollars. The rest of the book describes these investments in more detail.

Stocks

In America, we pretty much understand that the local dry cleaners or flower shop is owned and run by a family that has chosen this as their means to make a living. They invested their own money and borrowed from a bank to get that business started. The money they earn pays their business bills and the remainder is their income. We often call these "Mom and Pop" shops because they are owned by a local family.

But many people mistakenly believe that very large businesses and chains are owned by large companies. In fact, most of these large businesses are owned by millions of different people and businesses. Wal-Mart® is one of the largest retailers in the world. It is not owned by an individual or a family. It was started by Sam Walton in 1962 as a single variety store in Bentonville, Arkansas. At first, it was owned by one person who took out bank loans, just like many small stores in your local area. Sam Walton ran his operations so well that by 1972, he needed a lot more money to continue to grow the business. In 1972, Wal-Mart "went public," meaning that the owners decided divide their shares in the company into millions of smaller shares and sell those shares to the public. As of 1972, anyone in the world could own a small portion of this rapidly growing company.

People like Sam Walton benefitted hugely because public funds allowed the company to grow much larger than it could under his own personal ownership. He ended up owning a smaller portion of an extremely large company, rather than 100% of a very small business. The public benefitted because millions of people could become part owners in that very successful business.

Stocks represent partial ownership in a business. When you buy a share of stock, you essentially become an owner of a company. You have a claim to a fraction of the profits of that company, its assets, and its debts. As one of millions of shareholders, you can vote on how the company should be run and what it should do with its money.

Most people buy stock in a company because they want to share in the profits and the growth of something that is much larger than they can create or manage on their own. Wal-Mart® is divided into roughly 3,810,000,000 shares. These shares are owned by 1,362 large investment companies and by millions of individual shareholders. You can choose to join these people in their ownership simply by purchasing a few shares of the stock.

Stocks allow you to own a part of a business as a passive business partner who does not have to do any of the work to run the company. All of that work is delegated to company officers and employees.

Stocks are traded on an exchange where all potential buyers and sellers of those shares can find each other to make their trades. Most countries have at least one stock exchange; in America there are several. The best known of these are the New York Stock Exchange (NYSE), the NASDAQ (originally the National Association of Securities Dealers Automated Quotations), and the American Stock Exchange (AME).

Most of the big name-brand companies you are familiar with are publicly traded companies with shares you can buy on one of these exchanges.

Bonds

A bond is a loan to a government or company. Private individuals usually get the cash that they need from a bank in the form of a loan. You might use a local bank to take out a car loan or a home loan. The bank has enough money to make thousands or even millions of these loans while managing the money going out as loans and coming in as payments.

Big businesses also borrow money from banks in the same way. Sometimes, they need to borrow more money than a bank can loan to them, or they want to use the money for an activity that a bank does not want to finance.

When these and similar situations arise, a company can choose to get its money by creating a package of bonds that it sells directly to the public. Millions of individuals and large companies can then buy a small piece of this loan in the form of a bond. A bond is a connection between the borrower and the lender, similar to that created by the stock market. But with a bond, you do not own a piece of the company. Instead, the company owes you a portion of its future income.

Bonds are sold with a stated rate of return and maturity date. Just like your car loan, these loans have an interest rate and a final due date. The company issuing the bond will pay you interest every year or every quarter. On the bond's due date, the company will then return to you the initial amount of your loan. A bond operates very much like a bank certificate of deposit. Your initial investment is tied to that bond until it matures.

However, the investment market is just like a supermarket; if you need a product, someone will eventually create that product to sell to you. Many bondholders often have the need to get out of their bonds before the final maturity date. Therefore, a market was created to allow individual investors to sell their bonds to each other at any time. The prices they get for bonds depend on many variables, but the most important of these are the time until the bond matures, the rate of return for the bond, and the rate of return for new bonds with similar maturity being offered in the market. People will be interested in buying your old bond if it has a higher rate of return than new bonds being issued. When this is the case, they will pay you more than you paid for the bond. When the rate of return on new bonds is higher than the one you own, then other investors will pay you less than what you paid for your bond.

Bonds are more secure than stocks, especially if you plan to hold them until they mature. Holding them until maturity guarantees you a specific rate of return on your investment. If you want to sell your bond before maturity, the price you can sell it for fluctuates, as will your return. Since most people believe that bonds are more secure than stocks, they prefer to hold bonds when they believe that the economy and the stock market are going to decline.

Real Estate

Owning a home is a significant part of the American dream. It provides security and stability people cannot find with other possessions or investments. Your home and the land it sits on are your own piece of the planet. These establish where you belong and where you have power and independence. They also represent a coming of age or maturity. Home ownership says to your internal self image that you have grown up and have built a solid place for yourself in the world.

Home ownership is the first and largest step in investing for most people. They put more money and attention into their home than into anything else. Owning a home can be a 30-year commitment, which is longer than most jobs and most relationships. Your home is an investment that you make essential use of every day.

The value of real estate fluctuates just as any other investment. It goes up when demand increases and declines when demand drops off. In a growing and prosperous society, most investments increase in value over the years. Real estate has a unique place in the American economy and the American psyche. It is the one investment that almost everyone wants in his or her portfolio. As a result, there is a demand for it like no other investment. Additionally, the government has created a number of tax benefits that only apply to homeowners, and these encourage people to choose to buy a home rather than to rent.

Once you have your own home under your belt, you can also choose to invest in additional real estate. You can purchase an additional house for rent. You can purchase land for development. You can purchase apartments to rent in larger numbers. You may even grow your investments to a point where you can purchase commercial buildings or land for commercial development.

As a young professional getting started with investing, you will probably focus first on your own home and then on a rental unit. The universal goal of renting property is to collect enough money in monthly payments to cover the mortgage, taxes, and maintenance expenses. If you are able to do this, then your renters will be buying the property for you. In the short run, you may have no extra income from the property because you are using all of it to cover its costs. But the goal is to own the unit within 15 or 30 years without having paid anything except for the initial down payment.

Professor Robert Shiller, the Yale economist who co-founded the Standard & Poor Case-Shiller Home Price Index said that home prices in 1990 corrected for inflation were the same price as they were in 1890.

His argument was that real property ages and falls in value. *"Housing is a manufactured good and they depreciate,"* Shiller said. *"If they go up in price they will make more of them."* He added: *"Most people think they will go up in price; they are wrong."*

This did not take into account two factors: No more land is being made and land prices generally continue to rise. It also didn't take into account that with rental property, most of the purchase price is covered by rental income.

In a strong economy, you may find that escalating real estate prices and increasing interest rates will allow you to rent your property for more than your monthly expenses. In a weak economy, expect the reverse. Rental payments will not cover your expenses and you must be able to cover some fraction of them yourself.

As with stocks and bonds, there are certain risks involved when investing in real estate. We will explore several of these in the real estate chapter.

Precious Metals

Some people are uncomfortable owning stocks and bonds they cannot really see and touch like bricks and mortar. They prefer an investment that they can hold. In fact, they may want to hide it at home in their pygg bank, under a mattress, or in a deep hole in the ground. They have been convinced of the necessity of investing their money, but have not come to trust other businesses to hold those investments for them.

For such people, many different tangible assets exist in which they can invest. The most typical of these are gold and silver, usually sold as coins or bars. These traditional forms are meant to insure that the original content of the gold or silver has not changed, allowing the metal to be traded more easily. Gold bars held outside an official depositary must be re-assayed when you wish to sell them.

Gold, silver, and other metals really have no intrinsic value in the form of coins and bars. There is no shortage of gold for use in industry or jewelry and such businesses usually have a plentiful supply of the metals they need. The gold in coins and bars is almost never turned into productive items. However, over the centuries, such metals have gained psychological value across all societies and represent a solid item on which people have placed extrinsic value when other assets are losing value. Therefore, there is no reason to value gold, silver, or platinum other than for the psychological comfort they provide and the willingness of other people to value them for the same reason.

Collectibles

You may choose to invest in items that are rare and valued by others who would like to own them. These are similar to gold coins except that they are much more unique and difficult to duplicate. Artwork and antiques top the list of common collectibles but also include automobiles, coins, stamps, memorabilia, comic books, and a host of "fad" items.

Art, particularly from an artist who has died, exists in very limited numbers and therefore become rare items. Like a home, it carries two forms of value—the pleasure that you have in owning it and the value that comes from others who would like to possess it. If you enjoy owning and viewing a piece of artwork, it has value to you. But if others also appreciate and desire that piece of art, it has value as a resalable item. Famous artists like Picasso, Renoir, Degas, Warhol, and Lichtenstein attract the attentions of people with millions of dollars to spend. But there are lesser artists whose works can be traded by people who have only thousands to spend. These artists' value often comes from a unique style, subject matter, or audience.

There are dedicated audiences for paintings of lighthouses, wild animals, and American scenes. There are other audiences dedicated to paintings of New York City, Dallas, or your local area. Lesser artists strive to attract a following in niches such as these and build value in their work from those who compete to own them.

Unlike stocks and gold, collectibles require more careful maintenance and storage. Paintings and comic books must be kept at specific temperatures and humidity, and away from direct sunlight. Automobiles must be stored in a garage, driven regularly, and maintained.

A number of collectible fads have swept through every society. In the 1600s in Holland, there was a mania around owning tulip bulbs. The bulbs of specific breeds traded at prices equivalent to that of homes. Though the bulb itself had very limited value, it became the focus of thousands of people eager to own it and who were convinced that it was a way to make a great deal of money by trading it. More recently, the Beanie Baby phenomenon caused people to invest hundreds of dollars in stuffed animals that cost less than ten cents to make in China. The only value in these stuffed animals was that they could be difficult to find and other people were willing to pay to get one of the rare items. But tulip bulbs and Beanie Babies soon lost their magical attraction and their value fell to pennies on the dollar. A Beanie Baby that once sold for $200 in a collectibles store could later be found for 25 cents at a garage sale.

Collectibles are difficult to invest in because their value can literally drop to zero. But if you are able to get in and out early, you can make significant returns. Or you can be truly enamored with the items and enjoy owning and using them for decades.

Mutual Funds

Many people are not comfortable selecting individual stocks, bonds, or real estate. They may not have the time or feel they have the expertise to do it well, so they look for someone to select and trade for them. One of the most popular investments for such people is the mutual fund, which is a package of stocks, bonds, or real estate selected by a professional investor. In exchange for a fee, the professional endeavors to earn the best returns possible for those who invest with him.

Mutual funds are very comfortable entries into investing. A fund may own dozens or hundreds of different stocks or bonds. As a result, the failure of any one stock or bond will not wipe out an investment. However, the other side of the coin is that the explosive growth of a Microsoft or a Google will only modestly boost the fund.

Mutual funds provided by a reputable investment company are relatively safe and can offer a better return than bank savings accounts or CDs. Also, the professionals who manage such funds create offerings to match every investor's interest. You can purchase a fund the matches the Dow Jones Industrial Average, the S&P 500, or the NASDAQ. Other funds focus on specific industries, countries, investment durations, levels of risk, or specific accounting characteristics. There are literally more mutual funds that create unique investment packages than there are underlying stocks, bonds, and investable assets. In a market with 3,000 individual stocks, it is possible to create thousands of unique combinations. Given the popularity of mutual funds since their inception in the 1940s and their surge in popularity in the 1960s, this is exactly what has happened.

Mutual funds allow an average customer to hire a professional to manage his or her money with the expectation that the professional will make better decisions than the investor could, but with the understanding that returns will be an average across many different investments.

Derivatives

Finally, there are derivatives, investments whose value is derived from the value of another asset, such as real estate, stocks, bonds, or even indexes of investments. Rather than trade or exchange the underlying asset, derivative traders enter into an agreement to exchange cash or assets over time based on the underlying asset. For example, a futures contract is an agreement to exchange an asset like a stock or a bushel of grain at a specific price on a specific date in the future. The option to make such an exchange can be sold to others rather than held until the expiration date. This allows markets to trade an asset many times before the asset is actually delivered to a buyer.

Investors may use derivatives to speculate and to earn a profit if the value of the underlying asset moves the way they expect. Alternatively, traders can use derivatives to hedge or mitigate risk in an underlying asset by entering into a derivatives contract whose value moves in a direction opposite to that of the underlying asset.

Before you can invest in derivatives, you should understand how the underlying asset is valued. This usually means investing in the underlying asset for some time before moving on to derivatives. As a result, derivatives are often considered a more advanced form of investment that you should move into only after gaining experience in more direct investments.

Summary

This chapter has provided a brief overview of many of the most common and useful forms of investment you can use to build your millionaire portfolio. We will explore each of these in more detail in dedicated chapters.

Chapter 5

Patterns of Investments

In our success-obsessed society you might have been led to believe that all investments are designed to go up-up-up all of the time. But this is not the case. Investments come in a variety of patterns. Some are built like slow escalators. Others are like fast roller coasters. And others are like climbing a mountain or descending into a canyon. Each of these has a place and a purpose in society, business and your investments. But it is very important that you understand each pattern before you begin to use them to reach your objectives.

Consumer Goods

The most basic form of investing is the purchase of consumables and retail products. When you buy a consumable, you are investing in your need to eat, drive, and feed your daily needs. You have to invest in food, clothing, automobiles, electronics, and hundreds of other items. Each of these has a very definite value curve. The curve begins at Time 0 with the price that you paid for it. From there it declines in value because you use it or consume it. The best investments are those that you convert into a different form of value.

Food

Food is the most basic form of investment. You must purchase it to remain alive. The value of the food itself is the purchase price. But as you consume it, the food itself diminishes in value until it is totally consumed and has a value of zero. Within a single hour, your entire investment in food is gone. But the food has been transferred into energy that your body uses to think, move, and take action.

The goal of this investment is to derive more energy from the food than you spent getting the food. Or in other words, you should expend less energy earning the money for the food than the food itself will replace in your body.

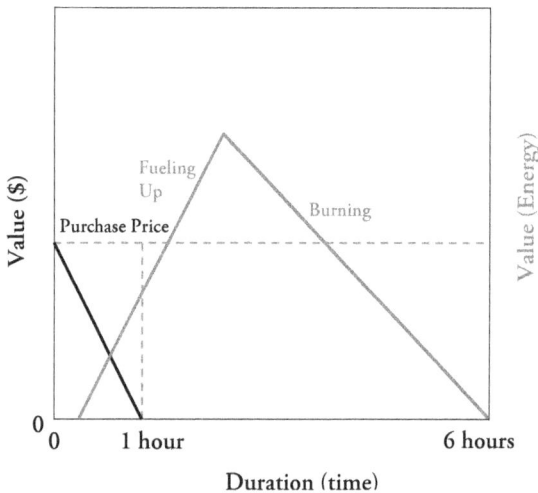

Figure 5-1. Value Graph of Food Purchase

In nature, the constant investment in food is the primary activity of the lives of animals. Their struggle is to expend less energy procuring food than the amount the food will replenish. When this does not happen, the animal or person will starve to death. There are numerous stories of animals eating low energy foods and filling their stomachs but there is insufficient energy in the food to keep their body functioning. As a result, they die of starvation, but with a full stomach.

This same kind of starvation can occur in humans. But for our purposes we are not interested in such extreme situations. We present the pursuit of food as a very concrete example of the importance of earning more than you invest in a product.

Clothing
Other retail items have a much longer life than a few hours. You may purchase them for a higher price, but they will deliver much higher returns. Clothing may allow you to interview successfully for a job. It may allow you to stand up in front of an audience and speak confidently. It may give you the confidence that you need to talk with an attractive person. It may allow you to go to work every day to earn a living.

In modern society, clothing is an absolutely necessary. Clothing also has value only upon its conversion into some other effect, like a food that provides "social energy" to function effectively. But like food, that social energy diminishes over time.

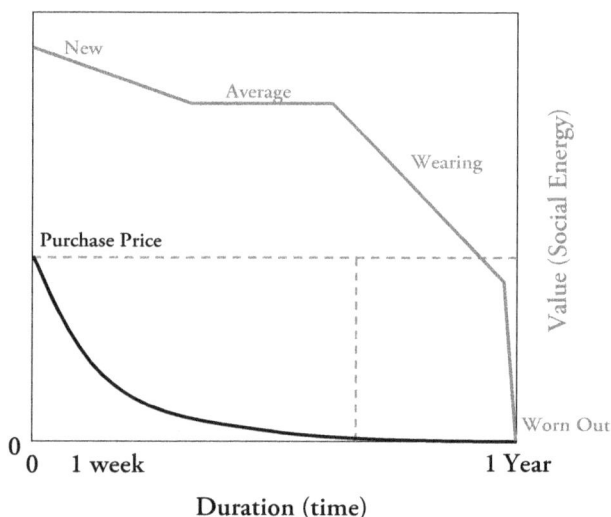

Figure 5-2. Value Graph of Clothing Purchase

The value of clothing diminishes to almost zero very quickly. After you wear a piece of clothing for the first time, it has almost no commercial value. You cannot return it to the store or sell it for a price anywhere near your purchase price. As you continue to wear the clothing, it diminishes in value until it reaches a value very close to zero. At that point, it must be thrown out, donated to charity, or converted into a lower form of production (like becoming a cleaning rag).

But the social energy created by clothing has a very high and immediate effect. Clothing is most valuable when it is new and first worn; it conveys its maximum message the first time you wear it and use it in social settings. After that, the social energy of clothing diminishes until it reaches a level at which it is just average attire that is no longer notable for how nice it is or how old or worn it is. At some point, the clothing gets socially worn and is notable for being a little less than average in appearance. From there, it continues to decline in value until it reaches a point where it can no longer function in society.

Like food, the value of clothing is in the conversion to another function. This is the typical value of all consumer goods.

Automobiles

The automobile is unique in society in that it can retain some or all of its value as it ages. There is an active market for used automobiles, while there is no such market for food. There is a market for used clothing, but it is much smaller than that for used cars.

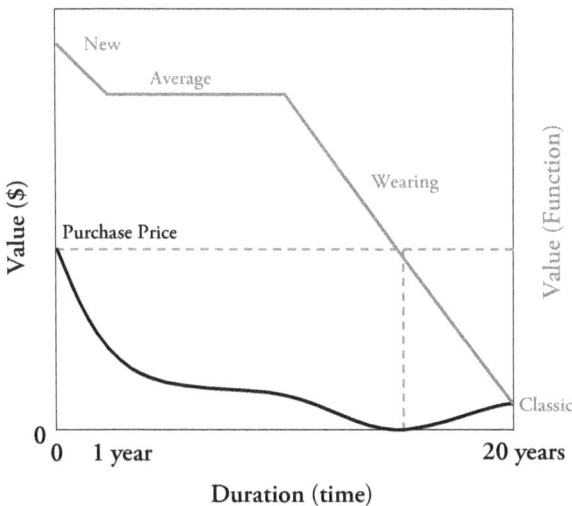

Figure 5-3. Value Graph of Automobile Purchase

The automobile provides transportation, mobility, and the ability to pursue opportunities that are in much larger geographic areas. As with clothing, the automobile conveys an initial social value in addition to its functionality. Over time, that value diminishes to something close to average and not particularly noticeable. The car maintains its average value until it begins to wear out and requires repairs, usually the year following the expiration of the warranty. From there, its functional value decreases. After about 20 years, many cars are considered classics and take on a value based on their age and rarity rather than just their functionality.

In any case, the value of the car comes from what the car can do for you, not from the inherent property of this metal object. Moreover, cars do not typically increase in value. So the investment is really a derivative. The primary value of the car comes from its function.

Real Estate

You can create similar graphs for everything you purchase. Items like food, clothing, automobiles, and education have a definite physical or social value in addition to their costs. Other items may create emotional value in you or in the person to whom you give it. But in almost all cases, these purchases have a very limited value as investments. The intrinsic value of the item diminishes over time. Similarly, the intrinsic value the item was converted into also diminishes, though hopefully over a longer time.

True investments are meant to increase in value over time. Their value may increase or decrease over time, but the long-term goal is for them to increase, as opposed to consumables that are meant to decrease in value.

Until very recently, most people would have told you the price and value of real estate always increases. The value of real estate has increased dependably for so many years that everyone forgot that real estate is an investment and an asset like everything else. When demand is up or supply is down, prices rise. But when demand is down and supply is up, then prices drop. For ten years, home loan interest rates have been very low, which allowed people to buy real estate and houses easily, creating high demand. That is the main condition for rising prices. When many people want a product its price can be held high. This is true for real estate, game consoles, and new cell phones. As long as demand remains high and continues to increase, prices will remain high. For real estate, this phenomenon also allows property owners to continually raise prices.

Real estate and homes hold a special place in the American mind. They are highly sought after as a form of investment, prestige, and luxury. This special place has allowed prices to remain strong and to grow for decades. Real estate has become an almost magical investment with mythical powers to grow. The general public forgets that prices can and do fluctuate. In fact, when you average out the ups and downs of the real estate market over several decades, you find that the existing increases and the sickening declines average out to a very reasonable 5% increase per year.

In real terms, holding real estate over long periods is an investment that pays better than bank deposits, but not as well as the stock market. In fact, real estate returns are similar to the average return on bonds over long periods. This certainly does not reflect the mythical position that it exists in most people's minds. There are two main reasons for that. The first is that many people buy and hold their houses for 10, 20, 30, or 40 years. Over such long periods, a 5% annual increase can compound into a very large return. Table 5-1 illustrates the appreciation in the price of a home. If you buy a home for $100,000 and hold it for 10 years with a 5% average price appreciation, it will be valued at almost $163,000 when you sell it after 10 years. That is a 63% improvement on the original price. To the average homeowner, this return certainly seems a lot higher than 5% per year, even though it is not.

Table 5-1. Effect of 5% Appreciation on a $100,000 Home

Year	5% Annual Growth	Year	5% Annual Growth
0	$100,000		
1	$105,000	21	$278,596
2	$110,250	22	$292,526
3	$115,762	23	$307,152
4	$121,550	24	$322,509
5	$127,628	25	$338,635
6	$134,009	26	$355,567
7	$140,710	27	$373,345
8	$147,745	28	$392,012
9	$155,132	29	$411,613
10	$162,889	30	$432,194
11	$171,033	31	$453,803
12	$179,585	32	$476,494
13	$188,564	33	$500,318
14	$197,993	34	$525,334
15	$207,892	35	$551,601
16	$218,287	36	$579,181
17	$229,201	37	$608,140
18	$240,661	38	$638,547
19	$252,695	39	$670,475
20	$265,329	40	$703,998

This picture looks better the longer you hold onto your home. At 20 years, your home could be worth over $265,000. At 30 years, its value tops $432,000 and at 40 years it is over $703,000. For most people, this is the best investment they will ever make in their lives. But it still reflects only a 5% return per year.

The second factor that makes the rate of return on a home so attractive is that most people buy a home with a loan and make at most a 20% down payment. Assume that their mortgage rate is also 5%. That means that at the end of 10 years, they have not spent $100,000 on their home. Rather, they have invested $20,000 as a down payment and have made monthly payments of $430, or $5,160 per year. At the end of 10 years they have invested in $71,600.

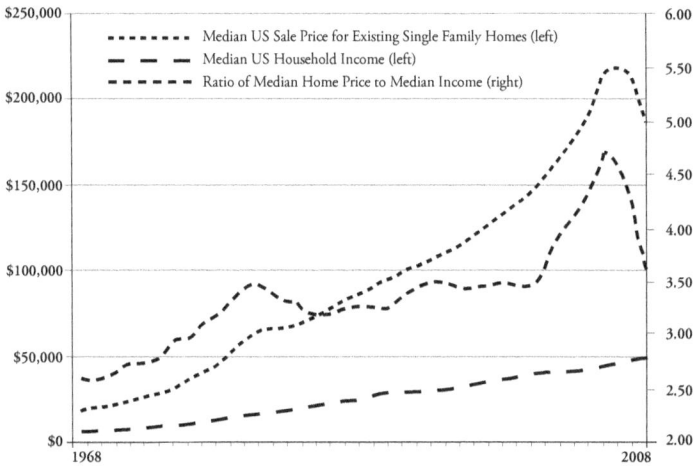

Figure 5-4. Growth in Home Prices versus Income

Starting around 2000, the rate of growth of homes and real estate started accelerating. This was tremendously exciting for those investing in the housing market from 2000 to 2006. The growth then flattened out, and in 2007 prices began to decline because fewer people could buy homes and many who had gotten in were over their heads and had to default on their loans. From 2007 to 2009, the market corrected itself and came closer in line with the average 5% growth rate.

Suffering in this roller-coaster ride was one of my neighbors. Her home was a nice two-story, three bedroom family home built and originally sold for about

$150,000 in 1992. In 2001, the original owners moved to New York and sold it for $211,000. They were happy with the appreciation on the home, but they missed out on the really big boom in prices that was about to happen.

In 2006, the second owners sold it to my neighbor and her husband for $375,000. During the middle of the real estate boom everyone in the area felt was way too high, but were thrilled to imagine their homes may have nearly doubled in value since the early 1990's.

My neighbor bought the house with a floating rate mortgage with a low initial interest rate and low payments for two years. But then two events happened at the same time. Denise and her husband got a divorce, leaving her to make the payments on a single salary. At about the same time the real estate bubble burst and the market value of the home plunged from $375,000 to the high $200,000's. She is now struggling to make payments on a house that is worth much less than she paid for it. After six months, she finally gave up. She moved out and let the bank foreclose on the house. She filed for bankruptcy to escape the creditors and hoped to be able to buy another house in a few years.

As a result of making many similar loans, her bank faced a number of similar defaults. The bank itself filed for bankruptcy. After two years, the once-beautiful house still sits unoccupied and unkempt.

Start a Business

A business, like every other investment, has a very predictable growth rate over many years. When a new business concept begins, it grows like crazy, increasing 100% or 200% a year. That is the pattern we all heard about for Starbucks Coffee, Dell Computers, and Google.

The first Starbucks was opened in Pike Place Market in Seattle, Washington in 1971 by two teachers and a writer. Their goal: to sell high-quality coffee beans and equipment. Now, less than 40 years later, Starbucks is the largest coffeehouse company in the world, with 17,133 stores in 49 countries, including 11,068 in the United States, nearly 1,000 in Canada and more than 800 in Japan.

Howard Schultz, now the company's CEO, joined Starbucks in 1982 as director of retail operations and marketing. After a trip to Milan, he suggested the company should sell coffee and espresso drinks as well as beans. The owners rejected this idea, believing that getting into the beverage business would distract the company from its primary focus. To them, coffee was something to be prepared in the home, but they did give away free samples of pre-made drinks.

Certain that there was money to be made selling pre-made drinks, Schultz started the Il Giornale coffee bar chain in April 1986. In 1987, the Starbucks chain was sold to Schultz's Il Giornale, which rebranded the Il Giornale outlets as Starbucks and quickly began to expand. Starbucks opened its first locations outside Seattle at Waterfront Station in Vancouver, British Columbia, and Chicago, Illinois, that same year. At the time of the initial public offering of its stock in 1992, Starbucks had grown to 165 outlets.

Much of the company's subsequent expansion has been as a result of acquisitions.

Starbucks, Dell and Google are exceptional for two reasons. First, they offered a new kind of business or product that was not certain to be popular. Many new ideas flop and we hear nothing about them. (In fact, some of Starbucks' ideas flopped.) But a few explode and they become household names. These successes do exist and we are all eager to find one of them for ourselves. But for every Starbucks success there are ten skateboard shops and fast food ideas that flop.

Once a company is established and attracts customers in its local area, it settles in at a relatively constant growth rate. For some businesses, that growth rate is 0% as they hold the same number of customers for decades. Their revenue increases only as they raise prices to keep up with inflation. This is the story of the neighborhood restaurant, the dry cleaner, and other service providers.

Other businesses aggressively add new products and try to get the same customers to buy more products. These businesses may grow between 3% and 10% per year.

When all three of these models are averaged together, the average growth rate for a business is around 3% per year. This figure also represents the average growth of the Gross National Product. Nationally, the country generates 3% more wealth from one year to the next. This wealth is not spread evenly. Some companies and investors reap 10%, 20%, or even higher returns every year. Others just remain even or lose money. When averaged together, the growth rate of businesses as a whole is 3%.

Stock Market

Investments in stocks have an average growth rate higher than that of either real estate or business ownership. Stocks are generally traded for firms strong enough to remain in business and attractive enough to get investors to want to share in their growth. Therefore, the stock market has a natural mechanism for selecting only companies that can and do grow. Companies that do not will fail to attract investors necessary to launch them into the public market. Most companies with zero or negative long-term growth are not listed on stock exchanges, which makes the average returns of the market higher than that of businesses in general.

In addition to this, the stock market is structured to get people to speculate on future stock prices. It encourages people to value a stock not based on what it earned last year but on what it might earn next year. This speculation and uncertainty causes prices to climb higher in good years and drop further in bad years. But the overall effect is that the stock market grows faster than the general economy.

Average stock market growth is from 6% to 8% plus dividends. In some years, this growth may increase by 20% or more and while in other years it will be down by 20%. Over the long haul, the market has increased between 6% and 8% excluding dividends.

Figure 5-5. Growth Rate of the S&P 500 Index

Figure 5-5 shows the rate of growth of a basket of stocks called the Standard & Poor's 500®. This basket was created specifically to help you understand how the market as a whole is performing.

Bonds

Companies, governments, and various other entities issue bonds as a means of borrowing funds from a wide range of investors who will each contribute a little bit of money. Legally, these bonds have a preferred, or senior, claim on the assets of a company. This makes them more secure than a company's stock. However, this security means that returns on bonds are lower than those you would receive if you took a little more risk on your investment.

In all investments, the rate of return is a function of the degree of risk that you take. When you invest in a bond, that bond is safe to the degree that the company remains in business. You lend the company $1,000 or $10,000, or more. In exchange, the company makes an interest payment to you every month or every quarter. Average bond returns are 3%. You receive this payment until the bond's maturity date, at which point your original investment is returned to you.

Every society gets excited about new products, new ideas, and new investments every few years. It may be Beanie Baby stuffed animals, pet rocks, or an Xbox game console. Sometimes these items go beyond their initial consumer product status and become investments. This happened with tulip bulbs in the 1600s and with Beanie Babies in the 1990s. The growth pattern for such items is always the same. Growth starts slow, then accelerates into a frenzy, and finally plunges.

These items take hold of the psyche of a group of people and create a value that cannot last. But in every case, those who are caught up in the frenzy cannot see the ultimate end. They see that a friend bought one at $10 and just months later it sells for $100. They are eager to get into this investment and pay $100 for an item they hope to sell for $1,000. Eventually, prices become outrageous, the music stops, and the balloon pops. When this happens, prices drop almost to zero. Those who stimulated the frenzy in the beginning make a huge amount of money. Those who get in early make a nice return. Those who get in late lose everything.

Rarity and the level of interest in society in artwork, antiques, and other rare items drive their prices. When society becomes interested in specific items, the price will rise significantly. But when that interest wanes, the prices will drop as well.

The value of rare items is supported by their rarity. They have this one advantage over fad items. Not only are no more of the item being made, in general the pieces that exist are slowly being lost. Antiques and artwork are lost in fires, floods, and other disasters every year. Some are simply lost or destroyed by their owners. Over time, their rarity increases, and this will keep prices high and may even drive them higher.

But a great deal of the value of these items is based on how many people are interested in owning them. When the economy is booming and people have a lot of extra cash to spend, they can afford to be more interested in artwork. When the economy is slow and even millionaires are going broke, then the market for these collectibles will dry up.

The goal here was to give you a quick picture of what you can expect in each category of investment. Each of these items has its own pattern of growth, decline, and stagnation. You have to make a decision about which pattern you can live with and which path you want to ride.

Chapter 6

Wading In

When should you start investing for your first million dollars?

Now. Today. Right now.

You cannot wait and worry forever. At some point, you have to start with what you know and learn more as you go. I do not recommend investing without learning anything. But I am urging you to push your fear aside and put what you have learned to work. You will never know enough to eliminate all your risk and all your fear.

Learning about investing is not like taking a college class. You cannot study enough to get all the answers right. It is more like a real job. You study, you prepare, and you jump in. You get some answers right. You get some wrong. But you keep learning and keep going.

When I started working and earning a paycheck, I was very comfortable putting my money in the bank. I knew the money in there would never decline and it was insured. I knew how the bank worked. My parents opened a savings account for me when I was 14. I put money into that account for years and watched the balance grow. I did not know much about interest rates, but I did know that the more I put in, the more I had.

When it came time to take the next step, I was very cautious. I wanted to make the perfect decision. I wanted to make sure that I did not lose one penny. I read my first book on investing and decided that I should find a mutual fund to start with. I searched a few magazines and picked the company with the best numbers in their advertisements. Then I opened an account with the minimum amount allowed. I sent them a check for $100 to open the account. Then I started worrying about my money. I was sure that I would soon be cheated out of my hard-earned $100.

My parents were no help at all. I had already gone further in investing than they had in their entire lives. They knew nothing about the stock market or mutual funds. I was on my own. In fact, a small group of new hires at my company was going through the same thing. We were all the first members of our families to venture out into this new world. We were all trying to figure it out from magazines, books, and advertisements. Soon, we gravitated to each other and began to share ideas. We pooled our ignorance and tried to give each other tiny boosts of knowledge and wisdom.

Based on their advice, I became comfortable enough to put another $100 in the fund, boosting my investment to $200. Then I opened an account at a second company, one of their favorites, and started with $100 as well. We each earned an annual salary of around $25,000 and were all worried about the fate of our $100 investments. We certainly were not going to go broke if we lost everything. But we had all grown up with "guaranteed, no lose" investment ideas, such as a bank savings account or a CD. We were not worried about the money having a significant impact on our lifestyles. We just had no experience with putting money at risk, at least not the money we hoped to be saving for the future.

All of us had college degrees and landed good professional jobs. We wore dress shirts and ties to work. We looked like the next generation of executives. But we had no education or experience with investing our money. Neither did we know where to go to get such an education. Our professional jobs gave us the income to start building wealth. The company encouraged us to join the 401(K) program, but only after we had been there for one year. Beyond that, we were completely on our own to figure out how to create and manage investments that would determine our level of wealth throughout our lives.

How to Start

Start simple and conservative. Start with what you already know and then move on to the next step. You have already learned the progressive steps from the pygg bank to the big bank to the stock and real estate markets. That is a simple roadmap for identifying your next investment. The chapters that follow provide a similar roadmap that goes from one level of investing to the next.

At first, you will have very little money. Your investment accounts will be small, perhaps $100 or $1,000. Losing this money will not do significant damage to your lifestyle or your retirement plan. But losing it will seriously damage your confidence and readiness to continue learning to invest. At this point in your life, losing $100 could be such a disappointment that you may retract from investing and spend the next 50 years holding all of your money in bank deposits. That would be a shame. A mistake using such a small amount could prevent you from earning tens of thousands of dollars over your lifetime.

When we counsel caution, we are not trying to protect your very small seed money. We are really trying to protect your confidence and your decision-making about investing over your entire life.

Many of us jumped into a sport or playing a musical instrument at a young age. While we were still getting our feet wet with all the activities and equipment involved, we encountered other kids doing the same, along with teachers and coaches. Our experience with these other people was the primary determining factor for whether we continued to learn and grow in that sport or with that musical instrument.

If the coach encouraged and provided instruction, we were able to build our strength and confidence. Over a few months or years, we moved from being totally inept at the sport to being proficient and able to compete. But if the coach was immediately judgmental, comparing us to all the other kids, and ranking us for immediate performance, then our experience was completely different. The latter experience can be so discouraging that we may give up on the sport before we even get to practice. We could see ourselves as terrible when we really were not terrible. But we never had the chance to find out whether we had potential, or whether the sport was something we would thoroughly enjoy.

When I was in the fifth grade, I joined the elementary school baseball team. I went to practices and quickly learned I did not know a lot about baseball. I did not know the rules, the positions, or many of the skills. In my neighborhood, boys did not play baseball. We rode bicycles, went swimming, explored the woods on the edge of town, built forts, and played dodge ball.

But we did not play baseball. That fifth grade team was my first experience with the sport. I was terrible at it. And the coach was probably even worse at his position than I was at mine. He just assigned everyone positions and let us play.

Our first public appearance was a series of three games against the town down the road. We all suited up and looked outstanding. My father came to the game to watch me play. I was extremely nervous because I knew I was still not very good at the game, but had improved since we started. My position for the whole first game was the bench. Several of us never left that bench through all nine innings. Then we played through the second game, and a few of us remained on the bench. Then we played through the third game. Finally, in the ninth inning of the third game, the coach realized he had not let several of us play all evening. He allowed each of us a turn at bat.

After sitting on the bench for three hours, all of us were stiff and cold. We had not moved a muscle in hours. Add that to the fact that we were pretty bad players to begin with and you can imagine the result. We each got very poor hits or struck out. We got two minutes of play before we got sent back to the dugout. Then the game ended and we all went home.

I was embarrassed and humiliated. I rode home with my father without saying a word. One of my good friends was the star pitcher for the team. The next day, I went to the coach's office and turned in my uniform. He swore that I'd have the chance to play next time. But I stuck to my guns and left. That was my first and last experience with organized baseball. Did I learn I was a terrible baseball player? Did I get a chance to enjoy the game and build my skills? No. This terrible first experience ended my interest in baseball for the rest of my life. I was done. There were plenty of other activities to pursue. I didn't have to waste any more time, energy or emotion on that game.

Investing is just like learning a sport. You need a positive opening experience if you are to continue learning, growing and enjoying it for your entire life. Our goal is to ensure that you get a good start so that you do not give up in the beginning and miss out on the benefits of a lifetime.

Start conservative and build from there. The beginning is no time to put all of your money in one "hot stock." You do not know enough about the market, the economy, or the company to make an educated investment. You might hit a home run and earn 10%, 20%, or even 50% in your first year with a hot stock. More likely, you will lose 10%, 50%, or 90% playing like that. Losing money might be a minor financial setback. But it will probably be a big deal emotionally and mentally and may be the last investment you make. This is the wrong way to start.

Cycle Warning

In addition to starting conservatively, I want to warn you about the cycles inherent to all markets. There is a period during which investors buy stocks and another during which they buy real estate. Then everything changes and they put their money into gold or bonds. All markets move in cycles that have major ups and downs. There are times when a specific investment trades very cheaply and begins to grow. You could graduate from college and start investing in those assets at the beginning of the up cycle and be successful without knowing very much and without trying hard. You will have come into the market at just the right time, purely by luck. You will have the best experience because you will learn and making money at the same time.

But this has less to do with your own brilliance and more to do with good timing.

Someone could graduate from the same college, with the same degree, and get a job at the same company, but just one or two years behind you. He could choose to invest in the same stocks or bonds or real estate that you chose when you got out of college. He could open his account with the same amount of money and even choose the same investment company to work with. But, because he started two years later, he may get into these same investments at their peak, after they had already gone through a fantastic two years of growth. Everyone working around him is talking about how well they did with a specific mutual fund or stock, encouraging the new graduate to get in as well.

But, because this person came in after two years of appreciation, that investment may soon drop 20%. For this new investor, that is a sharp confidence blow. The new graduate immediately lost 20% of his investment. For those who came in two years earlier, this 20% decline happened after they had already earned 40%. They still had earned a 20% profit on their investment. Both investors did exactly the same thing. But they had two very different experiences simply based on when they graduated from college, started making money, and launched their investing career.

Figure 6-1. Standard & Poor's 500 Index (1959 to 2008)

Figure 6-1 shows the pattern of the S&P 500 over 50 years. When you review past performance, you can see that the long-term trend of this group of stocks is upward. The S&P 500 looks like a great investment. But this is not how most people experience their investments. They go through daily gains and losses. They have no window into what the future holds.

If we take a snippet of this picture and zoom in, we start to see what the new investor experiences.

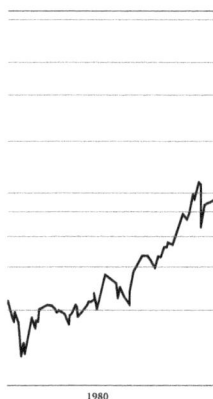

Figure 6-2. Short Term Window into Current Performance of the S&P 500 Index

If you started investing in 1985, you had a tremendously positive experience. Every investment you put into the stock market went up. You were a genius. You had the touch. You were giving advice to everyone you knew, including the new graduates who were being hired in 1987.

These new graduates joined you in your investments. They were encouraged by your stories of the prior two years. But both of you were new to the market. Your knowledge was limited; your experience was inadequate. As 1987 clicked along, both of you made some nice returns. But then in October, the market took a huge hit. It dropped more than 40%. The investor who started during that year was totally crushed. And the investor who started two years earlier lost a lot of his gains, but still had a small profit coming out of "Black Monday."

The difference between these two experiences was timing and the market cycle. One person was not smarter than the other. One person did not act more foolishly. The differences in experience were simply the result of luck. When you start investing, you really want to know what has been happening in a number of markets for the last five years before you arrived on the scene. You were not there to see it. But you can rest assured that those around you will steer you into the investments that have had the best performance over the last few years. They will put you "where the action is" or, at least, "where the action was" last year. Neither you nor they can know what will happen this year or next.

There is a cycle to everything. Nothing goes up forever.

If you jump in at the peak, a big drop will probably cause you to jump out at the bottom. You are starting your investment career by doing exactly the opposite of what you should be doing. You started by buying high, then selling low. We all know that is the wrong thing to do. But timing and emotions often force us into this decision. Then, after selling at the low point we are so traumatized that we cannot buy until all threats of another drop have evaporated. This means we wait until the market increases and everyone is excited again. Then we get back in. But we have missed the big run up that happened after the gut-wrenching drop. We have bought high again and are set up for another fall. If you start at the wrong time, then your experience and your emotions will put you out again at exactly the wrong time.

What happens to your investments in your first year will have very little impact on your overall wealth. But it could have a huge impact on your mental and emotional opinion of investing. Getting started right can make a big difference in what you decide to do for your entire life.

Depression Investing

Figure 6-3. Stock Market Depressions

This story mirrors the experience of investors who lived through the 1931–32 stock market crash that started The Great Depression. Investors who got in early saw their investments climb straight up for several years. But those who started in 1930 or 1931 were devastated by the crash. They saw an investment of $380 reduced to $42 over a two-year period. And if they decided to hold on until their investment came back, they were still waiting in 1956 when the market finally returned to where it had been in 1930. It took them 25 years to break even.

This traumatic experience defined a generation. Your grandparents and their children probably kept all of their money in a bank savings account or CD for their entire lives. They saw what speculating in other investments could do and had no stomach for it for the remainder of their lives.

If you are a young investor getting started, the best time for you to launch your investing career is after one of these terrible crashes. This way, the damage has been done to the market and to the investors who rode through it. But you will have missed it entirely. You will have the advantage of getting in when prices are low and most likely ready to start recovering from the crash that is ending.

Big Deal

Right now, your investments are small. Compared with the amount of money you make every month, they are probably less than 10% of your paychecks. Over time, that amount will grow. Eventually, you will have investments equal to your annual salary. If you make $40,000 a year, then in five or ten years you should have saved and earned enough to have investments of around $40,000.

At this point, the annual appreciation in your investments can equal your annual pay raise. You can effectively double your pay raise by managing your investments well.

In 10 to 20 years of investing, you should have enough in your investments that the appreciation in value equals your entire annual salary: you are earning one salary through your work and another through your investments. At this point, you really need to be serious about investing. If your investments can earn as much as your salary, they deserve at least equal attention from you or an investment advisor who can ensure the proper handling of this money.

It may seem impossible to imagine when you are just getting started, but many millionaire employees reach a point when they have to decide whether going to work every day is the best use of their time. Their investments make so much money they know that spending several hours a day working on them can earn them a greater income than going to work every day. I emphasize that these are not fabulously wealthy people. These are employees who have managed their way to millionaire status. These are people who started working in professional jobs just like you. These people are you in 20 years.

Choosing Your Investments

As we discussed earlier, there are literally thousands of different investments you can use, divided into a dozen major categories, hundreds of which you can access easily. Your choice of investments should be based on a couple of factors.

What do you enjoy? One of these investments will really interest you, while others will seem like a major burden. You will do much better working with investments that engage your mind and imagination than those you hate to think about or participate in. I have friends who love investing in rental properties. They are thrilled to find a house, fix it up and rent it out. It does not bother them at all to spend a weekend painting a newly-acquired house. All of this seems like miserable work to me. I much prefer finding a promising stock of a growing company. I enjoy reading about the company's business dealings and thinking about whether I can make money selling options on the stock. You must choose investments that interest you.

What do you understand? You must be able to understand how the market for your investments works. You must be able to read about them and know what makes them more or less valuable, and know when they are over- or undervalued. People who cannot understand how a stock operates may choose a mutual fund specifically because of this lack of understanding.

Where is the cycle? The time to invest in real estate or stocks is when the market is down. You do not want to get in at the top of the market and begin your rollercoaster ride with a giant drop. You want to get in early enough to enjoy the huge climb up to the top. If you cannot find a market that is down and ready to grow, then you might need to keep your money in bank deposits, CDs, and money market accounts until the opportunity comes around. No one likes to start by being so conservative. But this is much better than jumping in at the top, then losing money the next year.

Investing Experience

In the following chapters we will describe possible investments aligned with your level of experience. We will suggest investments that are right for you when you are at:

Entry Level—from zero to three years of experience
Intermediate—from three to ten years
Experienced—more than ten years of investing experience
Professional—investing as a primary means of income

There are no hard and fast rules that govern what you can and cannot invest in during your life. This is a crawl-walk-run approach to investing. It attempts to get you rolling and educated first, and then moves you on to more complex, risky, and technical investments.

Chapter 7

Entry Level…
Your First Three Years

W here do you begin when you are just getting started? What should your first investment be? If you are like most people, you made it through high school and college using just a checking account and a credit card. Neither of these was truly an investment account. They were really about spending your money, not about saving it and certainly not about investing.

The first step toward becoming a Millionaire Employee comes before even thinking about investments. You cannot invest without money so your first step must be about saving it. We have suggested earlier that you should pay yourself before anyone else and the amount you pay yourself should be at least 10%.

For some, that is easier said than done. You have student loans, a recent marriage or you are preparing for one, or perhaps you are buying or saving for the down payment for a house. There are car payments and payments you may not have made when you were with your parents or in school, such as electricity. You probably need more expensive clothes now that you are working. It can be tough to know where the money will come from if you are not already used to saving.

But unless you are unusual, some money dribbles unnoticed out of your pocket or purse just about every day. Maybe Starbucks catches some of it. Perhaps it goes for a soda. Or the local pub. Or comfort food while watching TV. If you were to think about it you might decide none of these things were important to you, yet you spend money on them. Do you even know to the last dime what you spend?

Here's a favorite way to track the money you waste without realizing it. It starts with a small pocket notebook that can be bought for a few cents. During the next 30 days, write down every cent you spend. Twenty-five cents for a parking meter? Write it down and do so immediately, before you forget. It will not make a lasting impression in your memory…and that's the point. So much for a can of soda? Write it down. Write everything down the moment you spend for anything. Don't leave it to your imperfect memory.

After 30 days, cross off every expense you cannot avoid: rent or mortgage payment, loan payments, utilities, car expenses—everything that is absolutely necessary. Make sure the expenses were for necessary things. For instance, gasoline to take your car to work might be necessary; gasoline for a 100-mile trip to the beach comes under a different heading even though it still goes on your list; it is not essential for your continued existence.

Be careful with how you account for food. Don't just enter "food - $143". That will be no use, as you will see in a minute. Write down every single item and its individual cost. Some food is essential, some is not; you will decide which is which.

Now you have a shorter list. Go through it again and cross off everything important to your lifestyle and enjoyment of life. Maybe this is where that trip to the beach comes in. Perhaps some food gets crossed off because you would be miserable without it. Sure, you could add these costs to your savings but if you tighten your belt too much it will become unbearable and your resolve to save will vanish.

Finally, you have a much shorter list. These are the things you have said are not essential and not important to your lifestyle and enjoyment of life. You, not some outsider, have said this is where you waste money that could be diverted to savings. These are things you will not miss and because you will not miss them your added efforts to save will be entirely painless.

Total the amount spent on this short list and make arrangements to have that amount deducted from your paycheck or transferred automatically from your main bank account every month or every two weeks when you are paid. Remove any temptation to spend it on toys.

Getting Away from the Credit Card

Another way to save is to avoid credit card debt entirely. The average American family has long-term credit card debt of more than $5,000. Let's look at what happens to the Dell family. They owe exactly $5,000.

Debt:	$5,000
Interest:	$83.33 ($5,000 x (20%/12))
Payment:	$150 (3% of remaining balance)
Principal Repayment:	$66.67
Remaining Balance:	$4,933.33 ($5,000 - $66.67)

If the Dell family never charges another penny on their credit card, they will pay a total of $10,600 over 15 years. The interest alone in that period will be $5,600, more than the original debt.

There is one thing wrong with this calculation: More debt is always added to these cards, even if it is no more than the payment made for monthly principal. Often, the debt continues for life or until the cardholder declares bankruptcy.

Part of your savings strategy should be to avoid credit card debt like a plague. If you already have some of this type of debt, get rid of it as quickly as you can. Borrow at a lower rate to achieve this if you must, but get rid of it. It is a financial cancer.

Saving money is admirable. But getting out of credit card debt is much, much, much better. *"Much, much, much"* means that eliminating credit card debt is at least three times as important as saving money in the bank. Even the richest millionaires need to be diligent about paying off their credit cards because the interest payments are such a huge drain on the nest egg.

Starting to Invest

Now you have a real professional job and are taking care of yourself, how do you start a real investment account?

Start conservatively. The government created several good investment programs specifically to help you get on your investing feet. You should grab the easy wins now and work on the harder problems later.

In the beginning, you know the least amount you will ever know about investing. This is not the time to play your hunches or to take hot tips from your friends. You know very little about how investments work, the history of real estate prices, or the effects of the economy and finance on stock prices. You should stick to the simple investments first. You will have plenty of time to get more complicated and take more risks as you gain experience.

401(k)

Ask your Human Resources department to tell you about any investment plans they offer employees. You are looking for a 401(k) plan or perhaps a profit-sharing plan you can get into. Most employers of professionals offer a 401(k) investment plan for their employees. These are tax-deferred plans that allow you to put money into them before paying taxes on that money. Your tax bracket is now probably around 28%. So that means you can postpone paying $28 in taxes for every $100 you put into a 401(k) or an IRA account.

When you do the math, you will find that if you put $100 in your tax deferred investment account, your paycheck only drops by $72. That happens because when you took that $100 as pay, Uncle Sam took out $28 in taxes. But when you direct $100 into a 401(k) or an IRA, Uncle Sam does not charge tax on the money, so your tax bill is reduced by $28. You are effectively investing $72 and the government is paying the other $28.

You will pay tax later, when you start withdrawing the money but at that time your tax bracket will likely be lower. Meanwhile, you have been able to make investment gains on what is essentially an interest-free investment loan from Uncle Sam.

In *Becoming the Millionaire Employee*, we call that getting FREE money.

People getting started in their professional lives usually underestimate by a large degree the effect taxes have on their personal wealth. Taxes are generally the number one largest expense that you pay every year. They are often larger than your home mortgage payment. They are larger than you car payments, and larger than the amount you spend on all your electronic toys. Anything you can do to reduce tax puts that money directly into your pocket. And you should choose to put it into your savings and investment pockets.

Both an Individual Retirement Account (IRA) and a 401(k) plan (named after a specific section of the IRS legal code) allow you to pay your savings and investment account before the government gets paid. And you get to pretend you never received that money. As far as the government is concerned, you did not receive that money this year and they are not going to tax it. So you save the money, and you get to keep the percentage of it you would have paid to the government as taxes.

Your employer creates its 401(k) plan. It is governed by different laws than the IRA. The primary difference of interest to you is the maximum amount you are allowed to put into this plan. Currently, you can invest $16,500 each year, a large number for most of us. This means we are allowed to put in just about as much as we can possibly manage.

Many employers improve on this by adding a matching payment. The law allows companies to make their own contribution to your 401(k) plan, another form of free money for you, if you just accept it. A typical contribution plan from an employer matches every dollar you put in with 50 cents of their money. The company will do this up to some maximum percentage of your salary. Many companies have chosen to match your investment in the 401(k) with either 25% or 50% of the money you put in, but only up to as much as 5% or 6% of your annual salary.

Under this formula, if you earn $50,000 a year, the company is prepared to add to your 401(k) contribution of $2,500 or $3,000 a year. If you put in $2,500, the company will match 25% or 50% of that, giving you another $625 or $1,250.

Given all the benefits of a 401(k) program, you cannot afford to miss out on using it. You put your money into an investment that will grow through your entire investing career and pay out when you are older and ready to use the funds. Uncle Sam gives you 28% of the money by postponing taxes on it, and your employer kicks in another 25% to boot. Even if the account in which you invest this money does not grow at all, you already have a 53% return.

Since the government and the company encourage you to invest in a 401(k), they share some responsibility for putting this money into a safe and appropriate investment. As a result, many company 401(k) plans allow you to put your money into a limited number of mutual funds. They have selected a group of funds they believe appropriate for your retirement investment. They likely also work directly with a specific investment company, which means you must use the investment company your employer has chosen. And you can invest your 401(k) money only into the group of mutual funds they have chosen for the plan.

This can be somewhat limiting, but it protects your employer from accusations that they lured you into investing and then allowed you or an advisor to invest your money into something completely inappropriate for you. The 50% boost that you get from Uncle Sam and your employer makes agreeing to these limits worthwhile. But your money will likely not be locked into this account for the rest of your life.

Most people change jobs every five to seven years. When you change jobs, you can choose to leave your 401(k) at your old company or roll the funds into a similar plan at your new company. Alternatively, you can roll the old 401(k) money into an IRA you control completely. Limitations that come with the current plan are only binding as long as you are with that company. You will probably have many more options for this money in a few years when you change companies.

If your employer has such a plan, your first step in becoming an investor is to use it to begin building your wealth tax free and to accept the 53% bonus money that comes with the account.

IRA

Unfortunately, not all companies offer a 401(k) plan. If yours does not, you can still access a tax-deferred investment plan in the form of an Individual Retirement Account (IRA). IRAs allow any individual who earns income to put a portion of that income into an account that helps you to avoid taxes, just like the 401(k) does.

Since the IRA addresses a different part of the tax law, the rules governing IRAs are a little different. Most significant to you is that the maximum investment is much lower. You can invest only up to $5,000 a year in an IRA, as opposed to the $16,500 maximum in a 401(k).

Also, since your employer is not involved, no one will give you a matching investment. You are limited to the free contribution from Uncle Sam of 28%. Still, this is a great deal to get you started.

You can open an IRA account at any bank or investment brokerage. Like the 401(k), an IRA is just a special tax-designated account. It does not limit what you can invest your money in. That is a separate decision. You will be responsible for choosing the specific assets to hold in this account.

Once you sign up for a 401(k) plan, putting money into it is automated. Your employer will direct the amount you specified into your account each month. You will see it as a line item on your paycheck and you will not have to do anything else to make sure the money is set aside every payday.

But when you create an IRA, you need to set up your own monthly invest-ment plan. The banks and brokerages managing most IRAs allow you to make automatic deposits into the account. You can select the day of the month and amount you want put into the account. I highly recommend that you do this. Investing automatically removes any temptation you will have to skip a contribution and spend that money on new goodies that month.

This is an important part of your future wealth and you do not want to mess it up by using the money on a new stereo or to repair your car. You'll be faced with many other expenses that could use that money. But you have to ignore those and keep putting that money into your IRA. Your lifetime wealth depends on it.

What do you do with the money currently in your IRA or your 401(k) ac-count? We will discuss that in the stock market section of this chapter.

IRA EXAMPLE
Let me give you an example of why an IRA is a great investment. Imagine that you earn a gross salary of $3,000 per month or $36,000 per year. When the IRS is at the front of the payment line, they take 25% of this, or $750. Yikes! That is a lot of money! Yes, 25% is one-quarter of what you make. That is a lot. I am sorry to say you will learn to get used to it. But I am happy to tell you there are legal ways to reduce that number. The easiest and best ways to get started are by using the IRA and a 401(k) account.

First, let's look at what happens when you are second in line to get paid, right behind the government. Let's assume you have decided to save $250 per month. For now, we will omit all other automatic deductions that come from your check.

So you earned $3,000. The IRS took $750. And you saved $250. That leaves you with $2,000 to pay everyone else in line, including those extra federal taxes that we won't talk about right now.

The IRA helps you improve this situation. Let's look at the same situation when you are first in line, in front of the government.

You put that same $250 in savings into an IRA. You earn $3,000 for the month. Then you put $250 into your IRA. That leaves you with $2,750. Now, income tax only applies to this number. Your monthly taxes are $687.50 instead of $750. Look at that! Your taxes dropped by $62.50. So you now have $2,062.50 remaining to pay everyone else in line. That $62.50 is FREE money, at least until you spend it. All you have to do is use the IRA to move your savings to the front of the line, before the government. And that is just in one month. You get to do that 12 times during a year, which adds up to $750 FREE dollars a year.

The beauty of the IRA? Everyone in the can US use it. It is open to absolutely everyone who has an annual income. You do not need any special deals with your company. All you need is an account at a bank or a brokerage company to get started. Also, this $250 per month is earning interest. It might be just 3% or $7.50 per month. But that interest is not taxed. If you saved that $250 in a regular savings account and earned the same 3%, the government would want $1.88 of that $7.50 as income taxes.

If you use the IRA, you will have at least an additional $842.70 in FREE money every year. For this example, I used a monthly investment of just $250. The law allows you to do this with up to $5,000 per year, which is $417 per month. If you did that, then the amount of FREE money you get in the first year goes up to $1,400! Now you tell me where else you can get someone to give you $1,400 for FREE. For most of us, there is no better deal.

Savings

The starting point for your investing accounts is when money first comes into your possession and looks for places to go. Most people deposit their paycheck directly into their checking account. They instruct their employer to direct deposit their pay into this account to get their money as quickly as possible. Depositing your paycheck into a checking account is not the end of moving and managing your money. It is just the beginning. A checking account is a convenient way to pay bills and to shop. But it is a terrible means to save and invest your money.

When I was young, my family used to join the neighbors for a long summer weekend at their mountain cabin. It was a beautiful, rustic cabin in the mountains of Colorado. We spent the weekend hiking, playing, and off-roading to some beautiful scenery. Since we were there just for the weekend, we brought all of our food with us. One of everyone's favorite items was watermelon for afternoon snacks and dessert. These were large, family-sized watermelons too big to fit in the refrigerator. So the challenge was how to keep them cold until we were ready to eat them.

The cabin's owner, Ira Pollen, had a trick he was proud of for chilling the watermelons. An icy mountain stream flowed by the cabin and he put them into the stream. If he positioned them just right in a side eddy, they floated there all day getting colder and colder. But the danger was that if you did not keep them out of the river flow the rushing water would carry the fruit away. Ira had plenty of practice and never lost a watermelon while we were there.

Trying to save money with your checking account is like trying to store watermelons in a mountain stream. It might work for a few days. But eventually your spending will carry away all your money like that stream carries away a chilled watermelon. You have to get your money out of your checking account before this happens.

As you start saving money, you should move some part of your paycheck into a separate investment vehicle. Many people like CDs offered by their banks. These are convenient because you can arrange for them at your local bank branch or through their Web site. These CDs reside in the same institution holding your checking account, so it is easy to take $1,000 from your checking account to purchase one.

The advantage of a CD is that it locks up your money for several months or a few years. In exchange for higher interest rates, you agree not to take the money from the bank for a specific period. More importantly, this money is locked up so the spending that rushes through your checking account cannot carry it away.

CDs are a great way to accumulate several hundred or a few thousand dollars. They allow you to set money aside and keep it untouchable while it grows. They are extremely safe investments insured by the government, meaning you cannot lose your money even if your bank collapses.

Money market accounts are similar to CDs. They work like a savings account but are governed by a different set of rules and regulations. The bank or investment company is allowed to invest your deposits into a much wider array of vehicles. They can earn a higher rate of return for themselves and can share some of that money with you in the form of an interest rate. The rate of return on a money market is higher than that for a savings account and closer to that of a CD.

Money market accounts have no lock-up periods, so you can move the money any time you want. These accounts are presented to customers as an equivalent to a savings account, but they are actually more similar to a mutual fund. You pool your money with other people to allow the bank to buy a number of different investments. In return, the bank shares a portion of their return with all of the people who put money into the pool.

You can open a money market account at most banks. You can also use it as the basis for your stock brokerage account. Stock brokerages use money market accounts in a manner very similar to the way a bank uses a checking account. It is the foundation on which all of your other investments are built. It is the first account to receive deposits and it is meant to be a temporary holding point for your money before you move it into the investments you really want to hold.

The money market account is the bridge connecting banks to investment companies. Both offer these types of accounts. At a bank, they are meant to hold long-term investments. At a stock brokerage, they are meant to hold short-term investments. This is where the two institutions branch off. What is long-term for a bank is short-term for a stock brokerage.

Stock Brokerage Account

401(k) and IRA accounts are most likely to be held by a stock brokerage company. Your company usually hires a specific brokerage to handle all the details of the 401(k) and to provide the investment vehicles employees can use. So, when you join a 401(k) plan, you will find yourself in the hands of a stock brokerage company. This may be one of the larger companies like Fidelity, Dreyfus, Vanguard, Smith Barney, Merrill Lynch (Bank of America), or a number of other famous names in finance.

If you work for a smaller company, they may have chosen a smaller investment company to manage their accounts. My experience is that the large companies can offer lower fees and better services than the smaller companies. Like Wal-Mart®, they have so many customers they can afford to sell their services at lower prices and make up for it in huge volumes.

When I Joined my first company and opened my 401(k) plan, the company used Fidelity Investments to handle these accounts. I think this initial introduction is the primary reason I have used Fidelity as my brokerage company for the last 25 years. I also found they were the service company for a number of my subsequent employers, so it has been easy for me to gravitate to them for all of my investing needs. As a result, when necessary I will use examples from Fidelity throughout this book. Other brokers offer the same services and fair prices as well, so you may be quite comfortable with some other company.

Initially, as a small investor you will not hire a personal "stock broker" to help you. You will hire a brokerage company with hundreds of people to guide you in making your investment decisions. These people are well trained to handle the thousands of people who are opening and managing accounts with their company. They cannot give you their personal advice on markets and accounts. Instead, they are trained to identify the category of investor that you are and to guide you to a specific group of investments that the company believes is appropriate for your category of investor.

If you read Money magazine, you will often see the pie-chart distribution of investments that are recommended for people at different stages life. These pie charts are designed to let you take more risk when you are young but become more conservative as you get closer to retirement. They contain a good mixture of diversity so that if one specific type of investment has a terrible year it will affect only a fraction of your account with the company.

In the beginning, we recommend that you listen to the advice of these brokerage representatives and allow them to point you to a small collection of mutual funds that match your tolerance for risk, your age, your income, and your interests.

A mutual fund is created with a prospectus that describes a specific investment philosophy, its objectives, and restrictions. This is the fund's mission statement. Beginning with a specific mission, the fund manager selects stocks, bonds, and other investments that will achieve the mission he has set out and that abides by the self-imposed restrictions. Every investment attempts to maximize returns for the investor. But all investors have their own ideas about how their money should be invested. Some feel all their money should be invested in stocks. Others prefer a portfolio entirely composed of bonds. Some like to invest in foreign countries, while others prefer companies only in the U.S. A few investors insist their money be focused in a specific industry. Everyone has different preferences. To appeal to these preferences, brokerage companies have created hundreds of slightly different mutual funds.

Many companies have so many mutual funds that they have created categories to organize those that are similar to each other. These categories include groups like:
- Domestic Stock Funds
- International Funds
- Bond Funds
- Money Market Funds
- Index Funds
- Exchange Traded Funds
- Sector Funds
- Real Estate Investment Trusts
- Age Targeted Funds

Within each of these categories are many dozens of unique funds. So within a single brokerage company you may find 500 funds available to you. There are another 500 at the next broker, and the next, and the next. There are literally thousands of funds to choose from.

How can you possibly choose from all of these? I recommend the following steps:

1) **Select a brokerage company you are comfortable with.** Do not worry about which one might have the hottest fund. They all mix and remix the same set of stocks. None of them can significantly outperform the market or their competitors.

2) **Let the company representative help you.** When you are ready to open an account, call the company and talk to their representative about your situation and your goals. Let them suggest several options for investing your money.

3) **Start with a money market account, an S&P 500 index fund, and a balanced fund.** If you want to remain as generic as possible, then select a money market fund as the basis for the money you transfer to the brokerage company. Then put all of your investment money into a fund that balances its investments between all of the stocks in the S&P 500 or balances its investments across stocks, bonds, and international companies. You are just starting so do not try to get fancy up front.

4) **Minimize your fees.** Every mutual fund charges a small percentage for the work they do. These fees are effectively the expenses and profits of the investment company. Some funds have unreasonable transaction fees. They charge you a percentage of your money to

buy into them, and perhaps a percentage to sell out. Skip these funds and look for something else. There is also the notorious 12b-1 fee, a fee for marketing expenses paid to attract commissioned salespeople. Skip any mutual fund that imposes 12b-1 fees.

5) **Don't buy losers.** In the mutual fund business there is a saying, "past performance does not ensure future success." Just because a fund did great last year does not mean that it will repeat the performance this year. But, if you look at the history of a fund and it has consistently performed worse than the S&P 500, then do not invest in it. If the fund has done poorly for several years, there is no reason to believe it will change in the future. You may not be able to predict which mutual funds will be the winners this year, but you can probably identify which will continue being losers.

6) **Keep learning.** If you read your brokerage company's Web site, you will find a torrent of information about a mass of different funds. You can read through this after you have put your money into a balanced set of funds recommended by the company representative. Over time, you will gravitate toward funds matching your style and expectations. But this can only happen if you keep reading about them.

One spring, I was lucky enough to be called to an event in the woods of Vermont. I flew into Burlington on a beautiful day and looked down on the woods, rivers and lakes of the state. At the airport, I grabbed my bags and a rental car and headed to the meeting. I arrived before noon and began looking for the organizers. They laughed a little and told me that the event did not start until 6:00 that night. That gave me several hours to work in my hotel room. Or... better, I had seen signs for a tour of the original Ben

& Jerry's® ice cream plant. It was just a 30-minute drive from Burlington, so I took off to enjoy the scenery and some ice cream.

I toured the plant, bought the T-shirt, and had a cone in the gift shop. One of the most notable features in the plant and gift shop was how happy and cheerful everyone was. Our tour guide told us that the break rooms were stocked with ice cream and that employees often enjoyed a pint over lunch or while on break. So, the key to happiness is a pint of rich ice cream.

This company creates some of the most original and odd flavors of ice cream that you have ever tasted. They are famous for Cherry Garcia® and Chunky Monkey®. They also sell Cinnamon Buns, Crème Brulee, and "Everything But The…"®. In addition to the flavors in your local freezer, there are a bunch of flavors in their "Flavor Graveyard." Those are flavors that never really caught on and had to be put out to pasture, including Tennessee Mud, Sugar Plum, and White Russian. The company keeps creating new flavors customers might enjoy. Some are a big hit and others head off to the graveyard.

Brokerage companies create mutual fund flavors like Ben & Jerry's creates ice cream flavors. You can have vanilla, chocolate, and strawberry. Or you can choose something with a mixture of stocks, bonds, and international stocks, but flavored toward the steel industry and avoiding exposure to Russian companies, but including just a little bit of the shipping companies that haul the steel to Japan to make cars.

They look for flavors that make money and attract customers. It is easy to create an exotic combination of stocks and it costs almost nothing to put it on a Web site for customers to see. As a result, there are literally hundreds of mutual funds within each of the large brokerage companies. Trying every one of them will not be nearly as enjoyable as trying every flavor of Ben &

Jerry's ice cream. Do not even attempt to do this. Instead, follow the six steps we listed above to get you started down the right track, and this will open your eyes to the excitement of investing.

Bonds

There are bonds and bond funds. A bond is a loan from you to a company or a government. It is just like your home mortgage in that you agree that the company can have your money for a number of years in exchange for a specified interest rate. The value of a bond is based on the rate of return it offers and the stability of the company selling it.

Bonds from the U.S government are called Treasury bonds or bills. These are considered among the safest investments in the world. Investors believe they will receive their investment back under almost every single adverse event that may occur in the future. As a result, these investments form the foundation of the American bond market. Prices for most other bonds are based on the price of Treasury bonds.

At this point in your investment career, I recommend that you not directly buy bonds. You should allow your brokerage company to include bond funds in your pie chart mixture of investments.

Beginning Real Estate

A lot of excitement exists around the topic of buying real estate. We consider owning a home, and then owning someone else's home, to be part of the American dream. We have been brought up to believe that home ownership is a great investment and that owning more than one home is even better.

Real estate investing is just like any other. Those who study and practice it can make a significant fortune. Those who dabble in it may make a little extra money. But both classes of investor can also lose everything they own by being too aggressive. We just went through a period in which a bubble in real estate prices crippled the economies of most of the world's leading countries. Prices for homes and land were bid to ridiculous levels.

People and companies borrowed way too much to participate in this market. When the loans could not be paid, there were defaults in the millions, and property buyers vanished. Either no one wanted to buy your home, or they wanted to buy it for half of what you paid for it. As a result, many new homeowners are stuck with a mortgage they cannot afford and a home no one will buy from them.

Real estate is not always a good purchase. You can buy it on sale. Or you can buy it at inflated prices. But it is never guaranteed to turn a profit. If you buy it on sale, you may make a killing by selling it to others when prices are hugely inflated. You will get rich and the buyer who comes later will be ruined.

As a Millionaire Employee, you work to make your millions from a combination of your professional income and your investments. You are not a professional real estate investor. During your first three years of investing, there is only one real estate investment you should consider.

At most, you should be thinking about buying the house that you will live in. I say "at most" because there are times when the real estate market is way too inflated and no one should buy into it. If there is a frenzy around real estate and prices have been soaring for a few years, then I would recommend waving off entirely. If there has been a crash, prices are depressed and banks are eager to make loans to homeowners, then you should be ready to buy a home.

As the saying goes, *"all real estate is a local market."* Prices, loans, and properties vary greatly around the country. What is happening in your state or city may be very different from what is happening in another state or city. You need to make your decision based on local reality, not the stories from places where real estate speculation is the official form of entertainment.

Here are some rules for making your first real estate investment in your own home:

1) **Buy where you want to live.** Choose a location and home you will be happy living in. This will be the base from which you will drive to work every day, be close to the shopping you need, mix in with neighbors you enjoy and select the schools for your children. Invest in the quality of your life, not in future profits from the property.

2) **Buy what you can afford.** Your mortgage payment will be the largest bill you pay every month. The size of this bill will determine what you can afford in all other areas of your life. Leave yourself enough free money to enjoy the rest of your life. I recommend a mortgage that is around 25% of your take-home pay. This means the first week's work each month goes entirely to pay for your home. Many real estate agents will try to steer you to homes that cost between 50% and 70% of your take-home pay. They will assure you that you can qualify for that size of loan, but you will be too broke to pay the rest of your bills. Do your best to find a home that costs no more than 25% or 30% of your take-home pay.

3) **20% down payment.** This used to be the standard for all home buyers. But banks learned they could earn a lot higher profit by lending you 90% or more of the value of your home. Most people still made their payments and the bank earned significantly more

profits. I recommend you try to pull together a full 20% down payment. In very expensive markets like California and New York, this is unrealistic. But for most other areas, it can be done.

4) **Live near your job.** If possible, select a home no more than a 30-minute drive from where you work. You will essentially buy yourself another one or two hours every day. The time you spend commuting is time lost every single day. It can rob you of many other things that you want to do. It will also separate you from your children's school, making it very difficult to balance your work and your family responsibilities.

5) **Do not gamble with your home.** The home you live in is not an investment you can afford to screw up. After you have bought something affordable, you need to work to pay down your debt on the house. There are many tricks people use to cut a number of years and thousands of dollars off their loan repayment. The two I like the best are:

- **Two Payments a Month.** Instead of making one mortgage payment a month, make two. Send in half a payment every two weeks. You pay the same amount each month. But by paying half the money two weeks early over several years, you eliminate thousands of dollars in interest.

- **Next Month's Principle.** When you get your loan, have the bank print your amortization schedule showing what fraction of each payment goes toward principle and what fraction goes toward interest. At the beginning, you will find almost all of your payment goes to the interest on the loan. When you write your mortgage check, look at the payment for the next month. Take the amount going towards next month's principle and add it to your payment this month. You will have effectively made next month's mortgage payment. You have moved yourself ahead two months instead of just one. At the beginning of a 30-year mortgage, this will be easy to do as it will cost you just a few dollars extra. In fact, the extra payment is so small that you might be able to tack on several additional months in principle without much trouble.

Summary

This is a basic investment plan to get started with. Your goal is long-term wealth and this is how you will collect and create the funds that are the foundation for that wealth. The 401(k) or IRA account is a great first step. Since it is not taxed, you have more money to invest. There are no taxes each year so your money grows a lot faster. Your employer might have a matching plan for the 401(k), allowing you to earn a great return right from the beginning and put more money into the account for long-term growth.

Many think of the 401(k) and IRA just as retirement accounts. It is the money they will live on in 40 years. This is the wrong way to think about this money. These accounts will be with you for your entire life. Because of their tax arrangement, it is difficult or impossible for you to take the money out before retirement. Since you are trying to build a portfolio of lifelong wealth, these accounts are the perfect match for that. For most people, these accounts, along with their house, form the basis for their entire wealth. A 401(k) and an IRA are lifelong wealth accounts, not just retirement accounts.

You may be eager to invest in lots of real estate. You want to buy your own home, and start buying other properties to either rent or to flip. During your first three years of investing, just stick with your own home. If the real estate market is in a normal cycle and prices are fair, get yourself a great place to live in and enjoy. An average American house is around $250,000. This is a big part of your investment portfolio. You do not need to put all of your money into one type of asset by purchasing multiple houses this early in your career.

Finally, welcome to the stock and bond markets. Open a brokerage account with an established company. Begin investing in a few mutual funds using the criteria we provided. Learn about investing in companies through their stocks.

And last but not least, a reminder about how much you save every month. You cannot build wealth by spending 99% of what you make and saving 1%. You need to develop a habit of saving at least 10% of your income every month and every year. This is the level required to become a millionaire during your working lifetime. A number of professionals save 20% or 25% of what they make. At that level, they will become millionaires during their 40s. They will have enough money to do whatever they choose, whether it is to continue working, retire to Hawaii, or focus on managing their own investments. Do not be afraid of saving only 10% when people around you are doing much more than that.

Chapter 8

Intermediate Investing in Stocks... Three to Ten Years

Your first three years of investing will fly by. As a young new member of your profession, you will work hard to become familiar with your job and your company. As a well-paid professional, you will try new things you could not afford to do as a college student.

During my first three years, I worked hard to impress my bosses with the work I could do. I also competed with my coworkers to prove to myself I was worthy of the job I had and deserving of a raise or promotion. It was a time of newfound camaraderie among people in similar positions. We wanted to bond with each other, become friends, share ideas, and still compete for raises and attention.

While this was going on, I also had time and money to explore new hobbies. I started wind surfing in college and was now able to buy my own equipment. I linked up with a club of young wind surfers at a local lake and learned new skills.

I purchased a nice touring bicycle and started exploring the country roads outside Fort Worth, Texas. Then I signed up for karate classes to burn off all of the excess energy I had after work. I took scuba diving lessons and took several trips to Cozumel, Mexico. Finally, I hung out with an adventure group that took monthly rock climbing, sail planning and scuba diving trips.

These activities will keep you busy. Investing will be just one of the many interests you develop. You will be so busy during your first three years you will not want to tie yourself down with so much investment work you cannot enjoy the fruits of your education and your new professional position.

But somewhere between three years and five years, you will notice you have accumulated several thousand dollars from your investments. You will start to notice shifts in the stock market have a real impact on your mutual funds. And it will begin to dawn on you that the money you have saved and invested needs a little more care than you have been giving it while you were out scuba diving, rock climbing, and bicycling.

In this book, I have suggested you shift from easy investments to investments requiring a little more work around the three-year mark. Some people will be eager to tackle more difficult investment decisions after just one or two years. Others will want to put this off until five years or so. Anywhere between one and five years is fine. Investing is a bigger part of some people's entertainment and interest area than it is for others.

Be flexible and make this shift when you are comfortable with it. But also make a mental note not to put your investment activities on "mutual fund autopilot" for your entire life. At some point, you will need to give your investments more attention even if this cuts into your adventure time.

Stocks vs. Other Alternatives

I chose to use the stock market as a means to build wealth. Other people prefer real estate or starting a small business on the side. These and many others are realistic alternatives. In this book, I teach you to build wealth using a plan I understand, and that plan uses the stock market.

The intermediate investment advice is divided into two chapters. The first is all about investing in stocks. The second combines a number of other investment alternatives. If you want more guidance on investing in real estate, bonds, or collectibles, I recommend you seek out a few books that specialize in this area.

You Lucky Genius

You are ready to start selecting individual stocks for your investment portfolio. Instead of letting a mutual fund manager pick a basket of stocks to average into your fund, you want to pick the single best one of all. You do not want to pick an average stock, which would be almost the same as putting your money into a mutual fund. You certainly do not want to pick a loser. You want to pick a stock that will perform above average. You prefer a stock that will have the highest return this year, and next year, and the year after that.

Luckily, this is easy to do. Luckily, no one else is trying to do this.

Of all of the people who have invested in the stock market, none have tried to pick the top performing stock for the month, the year, or the decade. None of these people have read the investment books you have read. None of them subscribe to the Wall Street Journal, Barron's, or Investor's Business Daily.

None of them have collected more information than you already have about your favorite company. They are not reading the company's annual reports or listening to the quarterly conference calls. They are not analyzing the financials of the company or the entire industry. None have hired professionals to help them identify the companies that are really going to prosper in the next year.

Luckily, you are the first person to come to the stock market with the idea of picking the best performing stock. You are the first one who will read about a company and analyze its prospects. Thanks to this situation, picking the stock that will perform the best will be easy.

No one else is working the way you are working, so once you find that top performing stock it will be cheap. You will be able to buy it at a bargain price. Once you have bought your shares, the market will realize its mistake in the next day or week. Immediately after you buy the stock, it will begin climbing. Its price will increase steadily every day over the next year. The stock you bought for $10 a share will be discovered by everyone else AFTER you have bought it. That will raise its price to $20, or $50, or $100 over the next year or two. You will double your money or better, and do it with great ease.

Another lucky situation is that you will have a few hundred dollars to invest every month from your paycheck. Each month you will be able to look at the stock market and pick out a new stock that is about to do the same as the last one. It will sell at a low price and be discovered by the rest of the market in the week after you bought it.

This will happen every month this year, next year, and for the rest of your investing career. When you are ready to retire, all the stocks you picked will have risen steadily every year by at least 8%. After 20 or 40 years of investing, you will have saved $500,000 or even $1,000,000 of your own money.

And, you will have invested it in the perfect stocks each month and that money will be $10 million or more when you are ready to retire.

That is the plan. Luckily, the entire investment world has set up this situation and is just waiting for you to arrive to take your millions from all the other investors. You will be given the red carpet treatment from the day you start until the day you cash out.

This is the investment picture you have in mind and millions of people before you have had in mind. This is the plan most people expect to follow.

Of course, it is that easy for a smart operator like you. Others may have failed at it. But you will pull it off just as described.

I hope you enjoyed this little fantasy. This is the only place the story will unfold like this.

In the Pits

In truth, the stock market is one of the most competitive markets in the world. There are more people trying to make their million in the stock market than anyplace else. Millions of people are already trying to do exactly what you are about to try. Some of them are incredibly successful. Some are terrible failures. Some are lucky. Some are unlucky. Your investment career will give you the chance to experience each of these outcomes.

The best guarantee for being successful with investing is to get in at the bottom of a bust cycle. Start investing after a prior bubble has burst and prices are at their lowest. Then, as the entire market grows, your stocks will grow. You look like a genius for picking a great stock. But actually, you just picked a great time to start picking any stock. Your stocks and all of those around it are rising on a wave of optimism, business growth, and global economic change.

Then, when things seem to be the brightest and most exciting, when everyone is jumping into today's hot investments, you step out. You recognize when the stock market has reached its top. You understand it can go no higher and you sell your stocks at their very best prices. You hold that money in cash, or move it into another wave at its the bottom as it is starting to rise.

If you can manage these two steps in timing, then you are guaranteed a great return on your investments. Luckily, no one else in the market is trying to do this. They are all just gambling like Las Vegas drunks at the roulette wheel.

Timing is just like picking a company. Everyone is trying to do it. Few succeed and many of those who do are just lucky.

Given this situation, you would think most people would just give up and let professionals manage their money. You might think improving your returns is beyond your abilities.

But professionals are bound by a number of laws and regulations that prevent them from using many investments open to you. Also, they also cannot take quick, nimble jumps from one stock to another and out again, which you can do. In most cases, they cannot accept a year of negative returns on a stock and wait for it to rebound the following year. As a result, they are constrained to follow a very common pattern that almost guarantees results very similar to stock market averages. The goal of most fund managers is to just avoid really bad investments that could pull them below the averages. Warren Buffet, the number one investor in the world over the last several decades, believes an individual investor can outperform the stock market if she simply uses her intelligence to study a company and select those with the best prospects over the long haul.

"If you are a know-something investor, able to understand business economics and to find five to ten sensibly priced companies that possess important long-term competitive advantages, conventional diversification (broadly based active portfolios) makes no sense to you." —Warren Buffet

You are trying to be the "know-something" investor who is looking for sensibly priced companies.

Select an Industry

If you will be a "know something" investor, you cannot just buy any stock recommended in the newspaper, on television, or in magazines. Such recommendations may certainly be for good companies. And many of them may be a good buy right now. But why are they a good buy? When will it be time to sell them? What economic forces switch them from a good to a bad investment? If you know nothing about the company or the industry you will not be able to answer these questions or make decisions about them.

One of the best things about investing in mutual funds is that you do not have to make these decisions; the fund manager will make them for you. Now, you are about to become your own fund manager. You will be the person who understands the company. You will be the person who gives the thumbs up or thumbs down to a decision. To hold this power, you need two essential ingredients:
- Knowledge
- Interest

First, you must have some knowledge about the industry and the company in which you are investing. The company has to be something you understand. It has to be something about which you can access reliable information. You are not a stock speculator who makes money off the daily or weekly moves of any stock. You are an investor who may hold the stock for months or years. You have plenty of time to get to know the industry and a few of the companies in it.

Warren Buffett has been adamant that he does not invest in companies too complicated for him to understand. He knows what kinds of businesses make sense to him and he restricts his investing to those. His holding company, Berkshire Hathaway, holds a number of companies that have clear business models and understandable means of making money; these are companies like:

Coca-Cola®

Fruit of the Loom®

Burlington Northern Railroads

Buffett has been very open about the fact he does not invest in most technology companies because he does not understand them. He does not understand how they make money and the forces that drive their industry. This caution has drawn a lot of criticism, especially during the dot.com boom. High flying investors criticized Buffett for missing the new wave of business, for missing all of the big IPO offerings, and falling behind the times. It is true that he did miss a lot of growth opportunities in companies like Yahoo!, Dell Computer, VA Linux, and Pets.com. But he also avoided the crash that followed.

Buffett did not understand these businesses and he would not know when to buy or when to sell. That lack of knowledge almost guarantees he, and you, will be invested in a company for too long. You will hold onto a company when it pops and when it drops.

You have to invest the time and brain power necessary to understand the industry. This depends on the amount of time and amount of brainpower you have. Some people can understand how an investment bank works, and some cannot. Some understand Coca-Cola® and some do not. You need to focus on an industry you understand, and one in which you can continue to learn and become an expert.

Second, you should select an industry in which you are interested. Since you will spend your valuable time and brainpower reading and thinking about these investments, they should represent a topic you find interesting. I believe this personal interest is important from both a subjective and an objective perspective.

The subjective point is that if you are interested in the industry and the business you will enjoy your time researching it. You will feel rewarded rather than punished by the study you need to do. The objective point is that when you are interested in a subject, you will spend more time learning about it. Your brain will be more engaged when you are interested. This enjoyment will multiply your effectiveness in learning about the company you are investing in.

Even though a company may be within your ability to completely understand, it may be so boring to you that you just cannot get excited about studying it. For example, Warren Buffett owns Fruit of the Loom®. They make underwear and other related clothing. Thinking about the competition in underwear sales and the price of cotton that impacts the cost of making the underwear might be something that you find either fascinating or completely boring. Do not invest in Fruit of the Loom® unless you want to spend your time reading about the production of underwear.

Knowledge and interest are complimentary characteristics. The more you learn about an industry, the more interesting it is. And the more interesting it is the more time you will spend learning about it. This also works in reverse. The less you know about something, the less interesting it is. And the less interested you are the less you want to learn about a subject.

Investing in Your Profession

As a budding millionaire employee, you are already working in some profession. You are spending 40, 50, or 60 hours a week living, working, learning, and breathing in an industry. If you find this industry interesting it might be one you choose to invest in.

If you work in the entertainment industry, you might choose to invest in movie and game companies. If you work in aerospace, you might want to invest in Boeing, Lockheed Martin and Raytheon. If you work in food services, you might want to invest in Sysco, McDonalds® and Darden Restaurants.

If you have a high level of knowledge and interest in your professional field this might be a great investment area for you. However, this is not an automatic decision. Some people find their own field too boring to spend their free time learning more about it. Or they are so overwhelmed by the minutia of working in it every day they just want to think about anything else once they are out of the office.

Finally, working in an industry can make you more pessimistic about it than you should be. When your company is cutting expenses, this can have a very direct and emotional impact on you. When you are an employee, it might mean you will be laid off. But when you are an investor it might mean lower operating costs and higher profit margins. You might find it difficult to separate your employee and your investor perspectives on your company.

There may also be an ethical issue with investing in specific companies within your own industry. If you work in the legal department of your company and are assisting with the acquisition of a competitor, it may be illegal for you to invest in that company based on the private knowledge that you have about the situation.

Finally, the potential exists that your income and your investments are two very large eggs in the same basket. If your industry goes through cycles of growth and decline, you might find your job is at risk at the same time your investments are at a low point. If you become unemployed and need to withdraw money from your investments to pay your living expenses, you may be selling your own industry when prices are at their lowest.

Just because there may be a number of issues related to investing in your own industry or your own company does not automatically rule them out as investments. These are just areas you should consider. If you find your profession so exciting you think about it every waking moment and you find yourself gathering all of the information you can about the business, then investing in your own industry might be the very best thing for you.

If you are ready to become your own stock picker, then you are ready to become your own industry picker. It is time for you to make your own decisions. My advice may give you some ideas to consider, but you should not let me make the decision for you. If you are not ready to make these kinds of decisions you are not ready to pick your own stocks.

Outside Interests

Everyone has interests beyond their own profession. We all do one thing to make a living and something else for entertainment and inner fulfillment. You probably have a number of activities that provide you with the two necessary ingredients for selecting a company to invest in—knowledge and interest.

If you are an avid cyclist you should find it easy to study companies that make bicycles and the entire field of use and sale of bikes. You will find the research fascinating and rewarding. It will help you select your own biking equipment and make investment decisions. If you are an avid reader you may know more about bookstores, online and physical, than most of the people invested in these companies.

When investing in these kinds of companies, it is important to think like the mass market rather than the niche buyer that you are. For example, if you ride a Schwinn or Trek bike you purchased down at the local shopping center bike store your tastes are probably reasonably aligned with the thousands of other customers who buy similar equipment. But if you paid $6,000 for a custom cycle you are in an exclusive category. There are only a few people who think like you do. Your goal in investing is to pick companies that attract more customers and earn higher profits, not those fixated on a very narrow or narrowing niche of the market.

I tend to have unique and rare interests in this area. The market around these interests is small, though they may grow over ten years. For example, I was very interested in nutrition and vitamins when this was a niche area dominated by ex-hippies selling wheat bread, yogurt, and vitamins. I had to order my vitamin supplements from advertisements in specialty magazines because no mass-market retail outlet existed. If I had been patient enough, I could have invested in General Nutrition Company (GNC) when it started and had faith its products would become a more socially embraced over the next 30 years.

Similarly, I became very interested in computer games in the early 1990s when there was almost no established industry. At the time, the number of people who had computers capable of playing these games was miniscule. Back then, we could not even imagine a business as large as Electronic Arts®.

Given enough patience, faith, and research, both of these areas could have been excellent investments, assuming I had chosen to purchase stock in GNC rather than Lee Nutrition, and Electronic Arts rather than Software Toolworks. That is where your research will pay off. You might buy your supplements from Lee Nutrition because they have the best prices. But you need to understand that GNC's franchising model was the right way to really grow a business in this area. Software Toolworks may have created the best games. But Electronic Arts saw the importance of consolidation and focused on purchasing companies that proved they could make great games.

This kind of understanding is what makes investing in companies as much fun as using their products.

Pros vs. Amateurs

If you are reading the investing press—the Wall Street Journal, Barron's, Smart Money, etc.—you will be exposed to information about every kind of investment there is. All these investments are not directed at you. You are not the only person reading these publications and they are trying to include information that will appeal to all their readers. If the investment does not make sense to you it is probably not meant for you. Millions of professionals are out there doing investment work that is far more complicated than you are attempting. Some of the information you read is for them. Do not try to act on every piece of good advice you see in print. Read these sources for information about the areas you understand. Don't try to pick a complicated investment out of a newspaper article and then wager $10,000 on it because the article sounded interesting.

If you hear about a unique form of investment, you need to learn more about it before you think about investing in it. You need to learn from books and online sources designed to educate you about the details of that investment, not from a newspaper. There are plenty of books and Web sites designed to help you. Use them before you make an investment decision.

Never jump straight from a new idea in the Wall Street Journal or any other publication into an investment decision. If you do not already know something about the industry, company or structured investment, the new investment is not defined well enough for you to let them have your money.

When I read a magazine article that recommends a stock, I might look into the financial history of the company to see if I am really interested. In most cases, I find the company would have been a great investment six months ago. It has gone up 10% or 20% or 30% from a very low point. By the time the magazine brings it to my attention, the profits have already been earned. In fact, the magazine author selected it for an article specifically because it was already a good investment for six months. With that as a beginning point, the author might suggest there is more growth to come. You almost never read about a great investment currently at its five-year low point on which the author is willing to bet his reputation the company is ready to go up 20% or 50% in the next two years. Magazine articles usually point out these companies after the big jump has already happened.

When to Start

In *Becoming the Millionaire Employee*, I recommended selecting a couple of stocks that interest you and watching them for an entire year. When you are in the novice stage of your investing career, you can develop a foundation of understanding of the prices and economic impacts on a few companies. When you are an intermediate investor, this is still good advice.

You can start investing today, but without much knowledge. Or you can pick a few companies and watch their stocks, read their reports, and watch the news about them for a year. Then at the end of a year, you can invest in a few of them, and with a great deal of knowledge. Which one of these sounds like it will lead to the greatest investment success over your entire career?

One of the great things about Western culture is that we are quick to make decisions and take action. We would rather make mistakes because we were too rash than miss out on opportunities because we were too cautious. Our society and our economy press forward constantly because we all lean in that direction. We all have a "go go go" attitude.

One of the weaknesses of Western culture is that we find it almost impossible to sit, wait, and think. The Eastern philosophy about taking action in its right time is a foreign idea to us. As a result, we are quick to take action before we have knowledge. We prefer to do something right now rather than waiting for a clearer picture to develop. When it comes to investing, you need to adopt the Eastern attitude of waiting. The market will be open today, tomorrow, the next day, and for thousands of days ahead. It will not close down tomorrow and distribute everyone's money. You have plenty of time to think before you act.

Selecting a Company to Invest In

Once you have chosen one or two industries based on your knowledge and interest, it is time to find a couple of good investments in each of those industries. How soon do you have to find these? Well, naturally, immediately. There are great bargains in the market right now. If you do not buy them today or tomorrow, they will be gone forever. You will have missed the greatest buy in history if you do not put your money into the companies that come to mind on the first day.

Of course, this is not true. But it is how many investors think and act. They believe they have discovered investing on the very day or in the very week that all the forces are aligned to give them the very best deal. That is crazy. You are more likely to have become interested in the stock market after prices have been on a roll for months, your friends are talking about how well they are doing, and you just cannot hold back any longer. This means that you come in at the peak of the market. Like jumping onto the peak of a mountain, what do you find in every direction? That's right—a downward slope. Once you are on the peak, the only way off the mountain is down. This is not where you want to jump in.

When you are ready to start investing, assume you have all the time in the world to read, think, ask questions and start slowly because you probably have a lot of time to get ready. The stock market is open every business day

Finding the right stock to buy is a lot like finding the right wife. You are not trying to find a lot of wives. In fact, you are not even looking for two. You just want one good one. When finding a wife, you take your time. You learn as much as possible about each candidate. You eliminate those who do not fit your style, your budget or your level of risk. Finally, you zero in on the one you really want and work your way towards asking the question.

(Well, that is what men think they do. They think they have some control. In fact, the girls decide whether they are interested in *you*. They charm you and you fall for the one that chooses you. You just *think* you had a choice in the matter.)

Take your stock out on a date, ask it questions, and watch how it behaves in different situations. Get to know it before you lay down your money for the engagement ring.

Learn Before You Leap

Warren Buffet likes to pick companies that he understands that have a strong position in the market. It is important that they have some protection that allows them to hold their position in the market and hopefully to grow. In fact, Buffett, the king of the value investors, has a few basic criteria for picking a company in which to invest.

1) **Industry leader.** Invest in companies that are the leaders of the industry. They are most likely to hold and grow their market share.
2) **Information available.** Invest in companies with plenty of available information on how they operate and how they earn their profits. Do not invest in "black box" companies that are a mystery.
3) **Understand what they do.** You should understand what the company does. If you do not understand it, you cannot make an intelligent decision about when to buy and when to sell.
4) **Strong management.** The CEO, President, CFO, and a few other key players should be people who have demonstrated they know how to manage a company profitably. They may have shown this at a number of previous jobs or in their current position.
5) **Reliable history.** Look at the history of the company. Does it have a reliable history of making products, delivering services, and mak-

ing money in the process? Or is its history like a yo-yo? Is it a constant up and down based on luck or the whims of the market?

6) **Promising financial future.** Is the world going its way? Are its products things you, your company and the world are buying and will probably buy more of?

I would also add Barriers to Entry to this list. Is the company in a business that is difficult for others to enter or difficult for them to get onto an equal footing? For example, in the computer market, Intel and AMD hold the lion's share of the business. It takes billions of dollars to get into the CPU business. This business will probably remain the domain of these two companies for years to come.

Getting Educated

Many people select a stock to buy in the same way that they pick a movie to watch. Their friend at work saw the movie and said it was really good, so they figure they should see it too. They saw an advertisement for the movie on television or in the newspaper and it looked really exciting. So they decide to see it. The movie has their favorite actor in it and they see all of his movies, so they will see this one.

In fact, this analogy is identical to how most amateur investors pick stocks: based on chatter they hear around them. But buying a stock is a much bigger commitment than seeing a movie. It also fills an entirely different purpose in your life. This approach to investing will get you into trouble. If this is your method you have either to change to a much more thorough method or to stop picking stocks and invest via index mutual funds. You have to stop thinking about investing as a popularity contest between stocks in which you try to buy the trendy, hot ones.

First, Learn

So how do you get educated? The first step is to gather information. Download and read the annual report of the company. Also read the latest quarterly report to bring yourself up to date. These two documents are audited statements of the financial health of the company.

You should also find briefings on the company Web site that are provided to analysts and at financial conferences. Page through these to learn the story they are telling major investors.

Then subscribe to a news feed about the company. You can do this through a number of online services. Your stock brokerage firm probably offers this service. You can also do it through Google Alerts and several other sites. You want to receive an email at least once a day containing news about the company. This will keep you current.

Read the Investor Services section of the company's Web site. This will contain several of the documents I recommend above. It will also contain summaries of the experience of company leaders, their mission statement and perhaps a map showing the major locations around the world.

Finally, you need to read the stock price information. Hundreds of online sites compete to provide valuable information about the company's stock price, earnings, etc.

Then, Analyze

Once you know what the company does, who is running it, how much money they make, how strong they are in the industry, and what their financial past looks like, you are ready to try to figure out whether you should buy the stock and how much you should pay.

Analysis is all about these two decisions.

- Buy: Yes or No?
- Price: How Much?

In determining whether the company is worth investing in, I recommend looking at some of these numbers:

- Return on Invested Capital
- Shareholder Equity
- Earnings Per Share
- Sales
- Cash on Hand

Look at the history of the company over the last three, five, and ten years to see if all of these numbers have been growing. Honestly, most companies cannot have all these numbers grow consistently every year. In fact, many companies cannot grow their financial position at all, but people continue to invest in them. Why people invest is an entirely different question we will not answer here. Simply be aware there are lots of companies selling shares in the stock market that no one should ever buy, but people still do. You will not be one of these people.

You are looking for a few companies that are good at their business and that have managed to establish a solid position for themselves over the most recent years.

In selecting a company, you want to select one that has shown it has the ability to grow its business faster than the rate of inflation. Inflation has historically been 3% per year in the U.S. Your company needs to grow faster than this just to remain even. Look for a company growing faster than 5% per year, and preferably faster than 10% per year.

MSN.com and Yahoo.com both have financial sections that contain a lot of useful data. You can use either one of these as a good place to learn about the company and to figure out how fast it has been growing.

How much should you pay?

If you have found a good company growing faster than inflation how much should you pay for its stock? Stocks are very different from consumer items. You can look at toothpaste, sweaters, and baseballs at the store and have a feel for what the average price should be. You can compare the qualities of each brand and choose to pay a little more for the best quality, or a little less for something not as nice but good enough.

The number of shares of stock that exist for a company is almost arbitrary. The more shares it has, the lower the price of one share. The fewer shares it has, the higher the price of one. The stock price does not tell you anything about whether it is a good deal.

When you buy a stock, you are buying a fraction of the business. More specifically, you are buying a claim on the current and future assets of the company. Current assets are reflected in shareholder equity. Future assets are reflected in earnings. You want to know how much of each of these you get if you buy one share of stock, which are reflected in earnings per share and equity per share.

Stock Price = Equity per share (Book Value) + Earnings per share

Let's use some real examples to illustrate this.

Table 8-1. Sample Stock Values

Stock	Share Price	Earnings per Share	Equity per Share	Price/ Earnings Ratio	Return on Equity
Apple Inc. (AAPL)	192.06	10.25	39.47	18.74	31.90%
Nike (NKE)	63.75	3.00	18.92	21.25	16.72%
Netflix (NFLX)	62.25	1.81	3.73	34.40	42.42%
Darden (DRI)	36.96	2.78	12.27	13.30	24.95%

Data as of January 31, 2010.

These four very popular companies illustrate the difference between the price you pay for a share and the value that you get for that price. It appears that Apple Inc. is much more expensive than any of the other three. But what do you get for your money?

For $192.06, you get a piece of Apple Inc. This means that you receive a piece of their offices, factories, inventory or products, and their bank accounts. When you add all this together and divide by the number of shares in circulation, you receive $39.47 worth of its assets. If you just wanted to use the factory to park your car, the offices to store your Christmas ornaments, the inventory to play your music, and the bank account to buy dinner, then this is a terrible investment. You just swapped $192.06 for a bunch of stuff worth $39.47. It would be like overpaying for something at an auction. But that is not how these assets are used. The company's assets remain in control of the officers, executives, and employees. They will use those assets to create amazing new products from which to make money. You do not want them to sell everything off so that you can get your $39 worth. You want the company to continue using its assets to make more money.

The second part of what you buy is the earnings of company. Apple® works hard to create products people buy for more than it costs the company to make. For your investment of $196.06, you are entitled to $10.25 of the company's total earnings. Apple® does not send you a check for that $10.25. Instead, they put that money to work trying to earning even more next year. You do not want $10.25 in cash. You want the company to use that money to make $12.00 or $15.00 next year. If they are able to do that, then the share for which you paid $196.06 will be worth even more to a new investor next year. The price of the stock will go up because next year Apple will have more assets and higher earnings. You will have bought the stock before this growth and someone else will be willing to pay you more for that share next year than you paid for it this year.

This sounds like an easy game. All you need is to find a company that will grow over the next few years, buy it now, wait for the price to go up, sell it at a profit, then repeat the process until you are a millionaire. Yes, that is essentially what you are trying to do. The reasoning is not that difficult. You should be able to pull it off without much trouble. You can think of dozens of companies you are pretty sure are going to make more money next year than this year.

So what is the catch?

The catch is that everyone else is trying to do the same thing. Millions of people are out there playing exactly the same game. They all try to do this at the same time. As a result, if one of them owns the Apple stock you want to buy, they also think the company is doing a great job. They will not sell the stock too cheaply. If they are going to let you have their share of Apple, they want to be paid a little extra for it. The price fluctuates every minute of the day because millions of sellers are being matched with millions of buyers, each with their own thoughts about what one share of the company is worth.

Since all companies have different numbers of shares, different amounts of assets, and bring in different levels of earnings, the share price of every company is different. You cannot compare shares based on price alone. This is why financial markets have created a number of ratios that try to standardize the price of a stock to facilitate comparison.

In the table, you can see just two of these popular ratios. The first, and most popular, is the price-to-earnings ratio. It is literally the price of one share divided by the earnings per share. Apple's price-to-earnings ratio is:

$$\text{Price/Earnings} = \$196.06/\$10.25 = 18.74$$

Apple is selling at 18.74 times earnings per share.

If you compare the P/E of all of the companies in the table, then Apple does not look like the most expensive stock any more. Using this measurement, Darden Restaurants is the least expensive; it is selling for 13.30 times its earnings per share.

P/E is not the only ratio that can tell you something about how well the company is run or how fast it might grow. Another popular measure is the rate of return on equity. Remember the offices, factories, inventories, and bank accounts that the company has? Some companies can make a lot of money with just a little bit of equity. Others require a huge amount of equity to make a little bit of profit.

Using return on equity as a measure, Netflix is the best company of the four at making money. They are able to make 42.42% in earnings for every dollar they have to work with. Netflix is essentially a shipping warehouse for movies. They buy and license DVDs from studios, then ship those DVDs back and forth among the people who want to watch them. This requires very simple facilities and few unique or expensive skills. But they are able to charge prices that give them very healthy returns.

So, which stock is the best investment? Is it the one with the lowest share price? Is it the one with the lowest P/E ratio? Or is it the one with the highest return on equity? Or is the best deal found in some other measure that we have not talked about?

Now you see why it is difficult to pick the best investment. It is not clear where the bargain is today. It is also not clear what the future holds for all these companies. Apple is incredibly popular right now based on its great products. But the company has had its ups and downs. All companies have. Your challenge is finding one that will become more valuable in the next couple of years.

How are you going to do this? And how are you going to do it better than a few million other people?

There is no magic answer to these questions. There is no secret solution to the problem. There is no way to be right all the time. Every investor loses money sometime. Some investors lose money all of the time. Your goal is to make more than you lose. Your goal is to make more than you could make without taking the risks of investing. If you can make more money with less risk by putting your money in a bank account, CD, money market, or bond, then you should do that.

The last thing we want to explain in this chapter is two of the major philosophies of investing. These two philosophies are similar to the Democrat versus Republican split in politics. Certainly, a number of other parties exist, but none are as dominant as these two. The majority of people are associated with one of these parties, and the minority follows some other philosophy.

It is the same in investing. There are actually hundreds of ways to make decisions about investing. But the majority of people fall into one of the two major categories, the value investor and the growth investor.

Value Investor	Growth Investor
• Looks for good products on sale • Looks for stocks with long-term growth potential • Plans to hold the stock for years • Focuses on buying at a low price compared with the value of the company • Is rarely influenced by daily or weekly changes in price	• Looks for any stock with momentum to go higher in a few weeks or months • Looks for a stock that market pressure will push up • Wants to get in right before a short-term growth spurt • Looks for profits within a few days or weeks • Plans to hold the stock for a short period

Value Investors

A value investor is a bargain shopper. He is looking for a company with a solid track record and good prospects for a long time into the future. He wants to find solid companies and then determine a fair price for a single share of the stock. If the stock is selling at about that price, then the value investor will wait until the stock is available at a better price. Given the fluctuations in the stock market, there are times when every company is "on sale." There always comes a time when even the best company is out of favor with the majority and its price falls. When this happens to a good solid company, the value investor moves in and picks up a block of shares.

The value investor is shopping for bargains. She does not have an itch to buy something right now. Instead, she is looking for a sale. She is learning about companies, identifying the strongest ones with the best future potential, and then buying only when those shares are available at less than their value.

A value investor learns about companies to get a feel for how much the company is really worth, and then to use that information to buy when it is selling for less than it is worth.

Growth Investor

The growth investor has a different perspective on the market. He knows all shares move up or down over a period of days, weeks, or months. He is looking for a company whose price will go up in the near future. He wants to buy into that stock once the growth spurt has begun, but when there is still more to go.

A growth investor seeks to get ahead of the pack. He also studies information about companies and keeps his eye on the business news for an item that will drive up the price of a specific company or an industry in the short run. The growth investor hopes to be able to get into a stock in the early phase of its growth and then sell it at the top of the cycle.

The business and investment press is full of articles with advice for the growth investor. You will read an article describing the great prospects of a company whose stock price has gone up in value by 20% in the last year. The publication will tout this as evidence of a good situation at the company and advise this company has room to grow even further. Once there is evidence of growth, the writer seeks to get people into a company before that growth is over. Of course, articles like this are often self-fulfilling because the advertising they give to the stock causes investors to buy into the stock and drive it higher, just as the article predicted would happen.

Which Are You?

Which pattern of investor are you? It is exciting to be a growth investor because you jump into all the popular stocks the press and your friends are interested in. You are "a player" in that you are right there with everyone else.

But being a value investor can be a little boring because you are usually buying stocks other people do not like and that have not made it into the headlines. You are deciding, often by yourself, that a company is underpriced and ready to buy.

Everyone has his own temperament and style. Everyone has his own way to approach the stock market. Most people are not purely a value or a growth investor. Most people practice a little of both styles. If a person is primarily a value investor, he cannot resist jumping onto an exciting and popular stock every now and then. If he is a growth investor, he sometimes sees a rock-solid investment that gives him the comfort of having a foundation under his dynamic growth investing.

In the next two chapters, we will summarize the investment methods of some of the more successful and popular figures in the world. You will see that each of them lean toward value or growth. But you must also realize that the public statements and positions of famous investors are crafted to make them sound more certain, more methodical, and better informed than the average Joe. In fact, even these people have trouble controlling their urges, hunches, and logical reasoning to remain faithful to their philosophy of investing.

Do not think just because you have trouble making decisions or sticking with a pure investing philosophy that you are too weak or too ignorant to invest your own money. You, like all the pros, are just human and subject to all the confusion that comes with using the human mind.

Chapter 9

Investment Styles of the Rich and Famous

$\mathbf{I}$f you are starting to invest, you probably want to learn from the pros how to do it successfully. You are likely to be eager to learn how the bankers at Goldman Sachs or the billionaire Warren Buffet invest their money so successfully.

Everyone has their own methods and their own ideas. There is no single successful method of investing. If there were, everyone would adopt it and it would no longer work. Buffet and others are successful precisely because they do things others do not.

In this chapter, we will summarize the investment methods of a few very successful investors. There are hundreds of others out there, all with their own views of market opportunities and their own methods. Some of those have been shared with the public and others are extremely confidential.

Peter Lynch, *One Up on Wall Street*

Peter Lynch managed what was the largest and, at one point, the most successful mutual fund on Wall Street. The Fidelity Magellan Fund became legendary for its ability to pick stocks and consistently deliver returns to investors. Lynch managed that fund so successfully from 1977 to 1990 he became the Jim Cramer of his day.

Lynch was hired as an intern with Fidelity Investments in 1966, partly because he had been the golf caddy for Fidelity's President. He was initially assigned to the paper, chemical, and publishing industries. In 1969, Lynch was charged with following the textile, metal, mining, and chemical industries, and eventually became Fidelity's director of research from 1974 to 1977. In 1977, Lynch was named head of the Magellan Fund, which had only $18 million in assets at the time. When Lynch resigned as the fund manager in 1990, it had grown to more than $14 billion in assets. From 1977 until 1990, the Magellan Fund averaged a 29.2% annual return.

Peter Lynch wrote three books on investing, including *One Up on Wall Street*, *Beating the Street*, and *Learn to Earn*. The last-named book was written for beginning investors of all ages, mainly teenagers. In essence, *One Up on Wall Street* served as theory while *Beating the Street* was about specific application of the ideas. *One Up on Wall Street* lays out Lynch's investment technique.

Lynch coined some of the best known mantras of modern individual investing strategies. His most famous investment principle is simply, "Invest in what you know," popularizing the economic concept of "local knowledge." This simple principle resonates well with average nonprofessional investors who don't have time to learn complicated quantitative stock measures or read lengthy financial reports. Since most people tend to become experts in certain fields, applying this basic "invest in what you know" principle helps them find good undervalued stocks in the products and services they use every day.

Lynch often said the individual investor is more capable of making money from stocks than a fund manager because he is able to spot good investments in his day-to-day life before Wall Street can. Throughout his two classic investment primers, Lynch outlines many investments he discovered before taking over the Magellan Fund. He found these ideas while out with his family, while driving, or while making a purchase at the mall. Lynch believed the individual investor could do this just as well as he could.

He also coined the phrase "ten bagger" in a financial context. This phrase refers to an investment worth ten times its original purchase price. It comes from baseball, where "bags" or the bases a runner reaches are the measure of the success of a play.

Roger Smith, *Becoming the Millionaire Employee*

My own advice is a variation on Lynch's "invest in what you know." I take this one step further and encourage you to invest in the very things you want to buy. You should control the urge to spend your money and choose to invest it in the companies that make the products you want to buy.

You hold onto your money by skipping one meal out, or a couple of sodas, or a pair of shoes. Do you like Italian food? Seafood? Steaks? Do you ever eat at the Olive Garden, Red Lobster, or Longhorn Steakhouse? These all belong to Darden Restaurants Incorporated (DRI). Darden has been very successful at creating attractive and profitable restaurants. With the money you have saved by turning down one meal out at a Darden restaurant, how about investing it in Darden stock? Instead of buying the food, buy the company.

If everyone is like you and eats at these restaurants, then the company should do very well. If you skip one meal at a Darden restaurant and its stock sells for $18 per share you can invest in one to two shares of their stock. Take the money in your savings or investment account and buy a couple of shares every month. If you do this, where has the money gone? Consider you ate it and it is gone.

If you think like that, it does not matter whether the stock goes up or down. You were going to eat that money at the restaurant anyway. Now, you own part of the company that makes the food you like. Continue doing this and you will soon have a nice nest egg made up of the companies that you do business with. I did this. I bought Darden stock in place of having dinner. I bought Apple stock in place of a new iPod. I bought Game Stop instead of a new video game. And I bought Exxon instead of the gas to drive down to the shopping center where I would have bought the other stuff.

Now I own a few shares all of these companies. And I got them using the money I would have spent on their products. If the stocks go to zero, I have not lost anything on Darden and Exxon, as I would have used up their products long ago. I may have lost a little on Apple and Game Stop since their products would still have been in my house. But, I am certain that over the long haul all these stocks won't go to zero. These companies sell their goods to millions of other people just like me and I believe they will continue to do so.

A note on stock purchases—it is a little expensive to place an order for two shares of Darden at $18. You will pay $36 for the stock and around $10 to the brokerage company to make the trade for you, almost a 25% fee for the trade. This is more expensive than paying interest on a credit card. Instead, it is better to put the money in a cash account and make one larger purchase at the end of the year, like buying 24 shares for $432. The brokerage fee will still be $10, but it will represent only 2% instead of 25% of the purchase price.

Michael Thomsett, *Winning with Options*

Michael Thomsett has published a number of very helpful books on investing, specifically on using options as investment tools. When he recommends options as investments he emphasizes you must stick with companies that are good investments on their own. Since the value of options is based on the value of the company, it is important you have an underlying vehicle that is valuable in itself. Also, since trading options can and will result in occasionally owning or selling these stocks, it is important you wind up with an investment that has value and provides a strong position in your portfolio.

THOMSETT'S THREE RULES FOR STOCK SELECTION

1. P/E ratio between 10 and 20
2. Companies paying better than average dividends
3. Companies that increase their dividends

Thomsett has three basic rules that he uses when determining whether a company is strong enough to justify buying options. First, he wants a company whose stock is trading at a price-to-earnings ratio between 10 and 20. This has been a traditional measure of value for decades. Companies trading at a P/E of over 20 are often considered overvalued, over hyped, and overripe. They have had a great run, but you can bet that the run is about to expire. When their burst of speedy growth lets up, their P/E will decline below 20.

Conversely, companies trading at a P/E below 10 are selling at a deep discount for some reason. The markets may expect the company to go out of business or perhaps it has been beaten so badly by a competitor that it will never recover.

When a company is healthy, its P/E will follow the average market P/E. It will shoot up on good news and drop back on bad news. Over time, it will tend to fluctuate with a P/E in the range of 10 to 20.

Second, Thomsett looks for a company paying better than average dividends. In a world where many companies pay no dividends, it might be difficult for you to imagine what "better than average" is. For companies that do pay dividends, a rate of 3% is often considered very stable and acceptable. In normal times, "better than average" might be 5% to 6%, or maybe a little higher.

You might wonder why a company would not pay a 10% dividend or even higher. Well, the answer lies in understanding the dividend and the P/E ratio. A 10% dividend refers to the cash payout based on the price of one share of stock. If a share is selling for $10, then a 10% dividend is $1. If a stock's P/E is 10, the stock is priced at 10 times its earnings. On a $10 stock with a P/E of 10, this means that the company has earnings of $1 per share. So, if the company pays out a dividend of 10%, it is paying out every dollar of its earnings as a dividend. If so, where does it get money to expand the business, pay for additional advertising, buy a new plant, or just increase the value of its shares? The company is spending every penny it makes in the form of a dividend.

In a world where the P/E of a stock is between 10 and 20, its dividend must remain below its P/E if it is to retain enough of its money to continue growing.

There have been times in the past when inflation was running at 12% or higher and bonds were selling at 12% to 20%. In such crazy times, an "above average" dividend was not as low as 5 to 6%. There were also times when bonds sold at 0.5%. When this happened, an above average dividend was not as high as 5% and may have been only 2 to 3%.

Thomsett's third criterion is an increase in dividends. This means companies are steadily paying out a little more each year than they did in the previous year, a sign that the company is doing several things well. The company is earning higher profits, which provide the revenues necessary to pay higher dividends. It is not borrowing a lot of money, which requires it to use its earnings to repay debt. And, it is confident enough in its ability to continue earning money that it does not hoard its earnings for a disaster on the horizon.

Information on a company's P/E and dividend rate are available on any financial Web site. For the third number, Thomsett uses the Dividend Investor Web site at **http://www.dividendinvestor.com/**

These three rules provide very common measures of a stock's past performance and the market's future expectations of them. They are not magic numbers, but understanding what they are and why someone might care about this information is very useful.

Christopher Browne, *The Little Book of Value Investing*

John Wiley & Co has published an interesting series of investing books called, *The Little Book of* .... Christopher Browne is the author of the volume on value investing, and he provides useful guidance. Value investors look for a company selling at less than its true value. They do not look for hot stocks that have a lot of energy, excitement, and hype behind them.

Value investors simply look for companies that are more valuable than the current market price.

BROWN'S GUIDELINES FOR VALUE INVESTING

- Buy stocks on sale.
- Buy when others are scared.
- Evaluate the worth of a stock.
- Sell stocks when others are confident and buying.
- Buy low, sell high.
- Buy positive free cash flow.
- Buy low P/E values, below 20, preferably below 15.
- Buy when interest rates are falling or are flat.
- Buy when Insiders are buying.
- Buy companies that have room to grow.
- Be patient.

Buy stocks on sale.

Stocks are just like goods in a store: they go on sale regularly. During one season, they are very popular and everyone is buying them. Six months later, they have gone out of fashion and everyone is buying something else. You want to buy your stocks when they are on sale, not when they are popular. Clothing fashions change every year. Swimming suits go on sale at the end of every summer. Stocks do the same. Their prices can vary widely over a one-year period. If you hear about a popular stock with a lot of excitement behind it, it is probably not on sale. It is all the rage. You should be more interested in the hot stock from last year or two years ago. This may be an excellent company that had a bad year and scared off all of the "fashion investors." It may have already recovered from the problem that scared everyone. It is on sale now, but once the market finds out it is still growing and is doing fine, the fashion buyers will be back. You have to buy your shares before the fashion shoppers arrive.

Stocks are not a consumer good. There is no reason to buy them when they are hot. You cannot wear them like clothing. They do not spoil like food or go out of fashion like clothes. They do not change model styles every year. The stocks you buy today are exactly the same stocks you could have bought two years ago, or someone else will buy two years from now.

The only fashion statement stocks make is when you can talk to friends about what you are holding. Owning stocks when they are hot might give you social cache. It might give you something to impress people with at parties. If you absolutely need this social cache, but did not buy the stock when it was on sale, then I can tell you how to achieve this without paying too much for the stock. It does not require any advanced trading techniques. Do this: lie about it! Tell your friends you bought 100 or 1,000 shares at a price that is 10% or 20% below where it is today. You get the cache, but you do not have to lose 75% of your investment when the "hotness" goes out of the stock and it drops from a P/E of 87 to 25.

This sounds harsh. Bragging about something when it is a lie is not very rewarding, that is true. But I will share a little secret with you. The stories you hear at parties about your friend's great investments… they are lies as well.

Separate your investment life from your social life. The two do not go together. Consistently successful investing is hard work, not lucky picks and hot tips.

Buy when others are scared

When the stock market drops 25% or 50%, most investors are scared out of their minds. They are certain the market is "going to zero." However, the best time to buy bargain stocks is after such a drop. This is when the smart money gets in. This is when the prepared investor scoops up bargains. This is also when the masses get out. They sell shares they bought at $100 for $50 or $40 and are glad still to have something left. They are scared their former hot picks will continue declining to $10 or lower.

When an investor sells a share for $40, where does that share go? It does not disappear from circulation. Another investor who considers it a bargain buys it. Which of these investors is right? Is it the buyer or the seller? There is no way to tell. But you need to know that even in times of crisis there are an equal number of optimistic buyers and pessimistic sellers. Otherwise, there could be no sale.

Evaluate the worth of the stock

When your stock drops from $100 a share to $40 a share, how will you know it will not continue declining to $10 a share? You have to know what the company is worth in real terms, not what the stock has done over the last five years. You need to know what the company owns. How much cash does it have? How much debt is it carrying? Is its value in hard assets or in goodwill?

Before you buy a stock, you must evaluate its financial situation. You have to understand what makes it valuable. How much should one share of the company sell for? The people who are on the buy side of a transaction during a crisis have done this analysis. They have a real appreciation for the value of the company. They are buying at $40 because they know the company is really worth $50. In some cases, they may have had their eye on this company for a long time. They like what it does and its promise for the future. But their analysis led them to believe the company was way overpriced. They have been waiting for its price to drop. They have been waiting for its "hotness" to wear off. This crisis is exactly the opportunity they were waiting for.

In this situation, you bought at $100 because the stock was hot. You were able to tell your friends that you owned the hot stock. Then, during a crash, you sold at $50 and lost half of your money. On the other hand, the value investor held his $100 in cash because he did not like the price of the stock. He had no exciting tales to tell at parties. But when the stock dropped, he bought it at $50 and got two shares for his $100 instead of just one. Then he went to parties and was told that he was crazy to buy that "loser". The owner when it was hot lost 50% of his money. The owner who bought when it cooled off paid half that price.

Sell stocks when others are confident and buying

All markets run in cycles. Everyone sells when the stock market is in the dumps because they have forgotten the good days when the market was increasing and when most stocks were overpriced. The market begins to doubt everything it believed about the companies, the rules of value, and the prospects for the future. Speculators become certain the world is ending for most of their investments and they need to hunker down. This leads them to sell stock to hold their money in cash or gold. This kind of thinking reflects a crazy mania. But it is truer than the fantasy the same people believed when stocks sold with a P/E of 87. If you can remain independent of both manias, you will be able to buy when the market is scared and sell when it is excited.

The time to sell stocks is when emotions have turned positive and everyone is excited about the stocks they own. It is difficult to figure out exactly when that is. In fact, determining when to sell in general is harder than determining when to buy.

Your can sell at a profit when everyone else is buying excitedly. But you can only do this if you first bought your stocks when they were on sale; if you bought them when everyone else was dumping them and the price was falling. If you were buying during the excitement along with everyone else you will not have enough profit to get out during the excitement. To earn really good trading margins of more than 50%, you must get into a company's stock when it is on sale. You cannot get in at the top, get out at the top, and expect to earn any money.

Buy low, sell high

This is the classic mantra of all investing on Wall Street, in real estate, with antiques, and other assets. Obviously, this is an idea that everyone believes and it is clear that everyone wants to do their investing this way. But very few make plans to follow this rule.

When you buy during an exploding market, you are already starting on the wrong side of the equation. You are buying high. Most investors fail to practice buy low, sell high. Instead, they attempt to practice two variations of this mantra:

- Buy High, Sell Higher.
- Buy High, Sell Low.

The hope is that the stock that has soared will continue to go higher and higher. The investor hopes to get out at a higher level. Some do accomplish it and make a great return. But most do not. Most investors cannot let go of the darling investments they are in love with. They do not sell higher. They hold onto their stock, believing that no matter what it has risen to, it will always go higher. These people only have one place to get out, and that is lower. They will not sell until their enthusiasm has been crushed.

Buy positive free cash flow

Cash is constantly flowing into and out of a company as it operates. It makes money from sales and pays for materials, salaries, and other expenses. The rate its funds flow out every month or every year should be lower than the rate at which its funds come in during the same period. If a company spends more than it makes, it will eventually drive itself into bankruptcy. It will spend all the cash on hand and then will spend all the cash it can borrow. At some point, it stops paying its creditors and there will be no more money to keep the company running. It will collapse.

Positive free cash flow means bringing in more cash than is being spent. In a simple business, this is a necessary and normal practice. More complex companies can bend this rule by offering shares, borrowing, entering into partnerships or engaging in clever bookkeeping. This may get them through a tough year. But if such practices become the norm year-after-year, even a large company can eventually collapse.

Buy low P/E value stocks

Buy stocks with P/E values that are below average. This means below 20, and even lower if possible. A P/E below 15 gives you even more room to earn profits when the stock becomes "hot" again.

Since we discussed P/E in great detail in earlier sections, you already understand why this is an important measure of the value of a stock.

Buy when interest rates are falling or are flat.

Interest rates are paid on bank deposits, certificates of deposit, money market accounts, and bonds. All these rates are linked based on the duration of the investment and the risk of the organization offering the investment. The rate of return on most of these is more secure than the rate returned by stocks. Therefore, the return you get from stocks must be higher than you can get from a more secure investment.

When interest rates rise, a number of investors will prefer the higher guaranteed rate rather than the rate they expect to get from a stock with its accompanying risks. They will sell their stocks and move the money into one of these more secure investments. Conversely, when interest rates fall, some investors will become dissatisfied with the return and move money into the stock market.

This behavior means, as a rule, stock prices drop when interest rates rise. And stock prices rise when interest rates fall. Both these movements represent just a fraction of the investing public moving toward higher rates and away from lower rates.

You should not buy stocks when interest rates are rising. If the Federal Reserve is raising rates every quarter, it will draw investors out of the stock market every quarter. Ideally, you want to find undervalued stocks and buy them when interest rates are high. These should get a boost in price when the interest rates drop again.

Buy when insiders are buying

Every company has a few leaders who run the company and are the first to see the results of their operations. They make decisions about how the company will invest and whether it will buy other companies. These people are in a much better position to know what will happen than is the investing public. They also know it long before the rest of the world.

These people have special restrictions placed on them regarding when and how they are allowed to buy stocks in the companies about which they have this insider information, but, they are not forbidden from investing in their own companies. Stock analysts watch closely what these insiders do with respect to buying and selling. The assumption is that they buy the company's stock when they know something good is coming and they sell when they know something bad is coming.

Each of these officers has their own financial issues, so they might sell because they need money for a down payment on a house. Or they might buy stocks because they are trying to buy a few shares ahead of one of their fellow insiders. Stock analysts try to separate personal needs from optimism or pessimism about the company's future. Analysts then try to use that information to determine whether the outsiders should also buy or sell stocks to match the trades of the insiders. Insider trading information is available on most public Web sites. Browne believes insiders sell for a number of reasons, but they buy for only one: because they are optimistic about the future. So he recommends buying a company's stock when insiders are buying.

Buy companies with room to grow

Everyone knows that Wal-Mart® is the largest retailer in the world. It is estimated that $1 out of every $10 spent in retail trade goes through Wal-Mart's hands. That makes it a great company. It is stable and secure in its leadership position. This made the company a great investment 20 years ago. But today, it is difficult to imagine that Wal-Mart® has any room to grow. Its current stock price is set at a value based on the revenue it earns now and the expectation those earnings will continue for the foreseeable future. The stock is stable but when you are the largest retailer in the world it is difficult to find new markets in which you are not already earning the maximum. Wal-Mart® may not be a great investment for future growth.

Investors look for small, young companies that will be the Wal-Mart® of the future. They look for a company with something special that will enable it to beat out competitors over the coming years. Such a company should have partnerships, products, technologies, or processes that make it special among the mass of competitors in the same line of business.

When searching for these types of companies, remember the advice of Peter Lynch, "Buy what you know." Since you use products and services, you may stumble onto something you really like, need, and will recommend to others. You are in a position to find one or two of these unique companies every year. When you do, take notice and do some research. It may be the next Wal-Mart®.

Be patient

Be patient. Wait. Think. Think again. Choose to do nothing.

Do not constantly shift your money from one stock to another. Do not sell a stock when it declines 10% from the price at which you bought it. Think about what the company is worth. Consider buying more instead of selling. Avoid the buy high, sell low trap by waiting.

If you have cash, do not be in a hurry to spend it on stocks if this is not the right time. Bide your time. Wait for the price to come down. Wait for the opportunities that we described earlier. The stock market will not close tomorrow. The companies you are interested in will still be trading 10 years from now. Be patient. If you buy them at the right time, you will make money. If you buy the same companies at the wrong time, you will lose money. Do not be so quick to judge you made a mistake and need to pursue something different. Your choices may have been 100% correct, but your timing may have been a little too soon.

If a stock is championed in the press, you know that millions of others are aware of it as well. These millions share the same information about the company from the article. To some degree they will all think alike. And they will all act alike. The stock will probably get a little boost from this free advertising. But then the effect will probably wear off and the price will settle back to a lower level. If you can wait a few days, you will probably get a better price.

These are just a few of the guiding principles Browne discusses in his book. He has a lot more to say in such a little book. But these provide great perspective on what makes a stock the right one at the right time.

Warren Buffet, from *The Warren Buffet Way* by Robert Hagstrom

Warren Buffett is the biggest rock star in investing. He is the one name and face that almost everyone recognizes. Buffett has been part of the investing landscape for sixty years and has been consistently successful. As a result, everyone wants to know his secret for successful investing. Hundreds of news articles and at least one book are written about him every year. The funny thing is that Buffett has never hidden his secret. He has been consistently open about how he selects his investments and what he avoids. His strategy is captured over and over in article after article and book after book. In theory, you could pick up just one of these books, read it, and have your strategy for investing. However, in practice, Buffett's strategy is too simple for most people to accept. Everyone is eager to hear about his "trick." What does he have up his sleeve that he is not sharing?

Buffett himself believes any above-average investor can be successful at picking his or her own stocks. He recommends stocks as a better option than mutual funds if you are willing do the work to evaluate companies and their value as represented in the stock price.

"If you are a know-something investor, able to understand business economics and to find five to ten sensibly priced companies that possess important long-term competitive advantages, conventional diversification makes no sense for you."—Warren Buffet, Berkshire Hathaway Annual Report, 1993.

"With each investment you make, you should have the courage and conviction to place at least 10 percent of your net worth in that stock" — Warren Buffet

Buffett sees the entire market as a single personal investor who is willing to buy or sell a stock at a different price from one day to the next. He calls this investor "Mr. Market," a fictional character who represents the crazy, moody, over reactive behavior of the mass of investors. Mr. Market might get excited about a stock one month and drive the price for it from $50 to $100 based on news, rumors, new technologies, or just a hunch. When that hunch does not come to fruition in a month of two, Mr. Market might get depressed and let the price of the stock fall right back to $50. Buffett insists you must not think like Mr. Market. You must not believe his moods, good or bad, are a reliable measure of the value of a stock. You have to study, think, and act on your own.

If you are a lemming who believes everything the masses believe you will follow the crowd's up and down moods. However, a moody investor is a looser investor. Your mood is good when a stock is up, so you buy it at the top. Your mood is bad when a stock is down, so you sell at the bottom.

Buffett tries to separate himself from the market lemmings chasing the same news about the same stocks.

Buffett believes in reading, reading, and reading about companies, industries, economies, and world trends. He spends hours, days, and weeks with reports on the performance of these entities. He builds for himself a picture of the core value of a company. Once you know the core value of a company, you can recognize when it is selling below that price or above that price. This is the guidance he uses to decide which companies to buy and at what price.

Buffett does not buy based on the excitement of the market. He buys based on his own understanding of the value of a company and his projection of what it will be worth in the future. His analysis of companies is not always simple; it is thorough and attempts to be objective. It avoids the hype Wall Street likes to generate around specific companies at specific times.

Business Tenets

> Is the business simple and understandable?
> Does the business have a consistent operating history?
> Does the business have favorable long-term prospects?

If you plan to invest in a company, you have to understand what the company does to earn its money. If you do not understand this, you are not in a position to make decisions about when to buy or when to sell. Thousands of companies are available in the market. You should stick to those you can understand. Leave the others for people who have a different kind of expertise.

Look at the company's history. Has it been successful over the long run? Does it have several years of successful operations that tell you it knows what it is doing and has been able to create competitive products or services? If its earnings look like the jagged edge of a saw with no upward trend, the company will not be a good investment.

Many companies have been successful in expanding their business, but may have reached the end of that growth. They may have grown as large as they can, have built the best product they can manage, or have lived past the market's demand for the product. Can you determine whether the market will continue to purchase their products and whether those purchases will increase or decrease in the future?

Management Tenets

> Is management rational?
> Is management candid with its shareholders?
> Does management resist the institutional imperative?

A company's management speaks to shareholders in annual reports, on investor teleconferences, through news releases, and at professional meetings. Seek out the statements by the CEO, president, CFO, and other senior leaders. As you read their statements, do the leaders sound like they have the best interests of their shareholders in mind? Are they speaking candidly or are their statements vague, confusing, or misleading? Have past public statements proven to be accurate or have they been unveiled as wrong or misleading?

When you invest in a company, you become a junior partner with these leaders in running the company. You need to determine whether the leaders are the kinds of people you should trust with your money.

The institutional imperative is the requirement of the company to act in the best interests of the owners (shareholders) and to return to these owners a respectable and fair profit on their investment. Not all corporate leaders do this or even believe in this. Your research must try to determine what the leaders of a company believe is their responsibility to the real owners of a company.

Financial Tenets

> Focus on Return on Equity
> Calculate "Owner Earnings"
> Look for companies with high profit margins
> For every dollar retained, make sure that the company
> has created at least one dollar of market value

The third set of criteria focuses on the financials of the company. What kind of return does the company generate? For every dollar of existing shareholder equity, how much return (or income) does it generate? This ratio indicates how expensive it is to earn a dollar of income. Some companies have very low overhead for generating revenue, while others require significant investments to make the business work. For example, the local lawn boy can run his business with an investment in a mower and some gasoline. But the newspaper delivery person has to buy a car and a larger amount of gasoline to operate his business. A more expensive business needs to generate higher levels of income to justify the amount of investment required to run the company. Since comparing the income from a lawn service with that of a newspaper service does not capture the differences in investment required, it is better to compare companies based on the return on equity ratio, which helps normalize the information.

Companies also differ greatly in their ability to generate a profit. Many companies generate negative income for many years. When this happens, the company may be headed for the trash heap, and may be about to go out of business. Alternatively, it could be experiencing a temporary dip in its market. Or it may be spending money to get itself ready for a big breakout in the near future. If profits are negative, you need to know the reason. Is the company failing compared with its competitors? Is the entire industry segment in a slump? Or is the company getting ready for something big? Those who know this information make the right decision, while those who do not are guessing or gambling.

Companies earning a profit may have a 5% profit margin or a 25% profit margin. For example, a restaurant has costs associated with every meal it serves, such as the cost of the food to make that meal. An online music store has a fixed cost of acquiring a song to sell, and its marginal cost to deliver each copy of that song to a customer is almost zero. So the online store has the potential to earn much higher profits. This same model works in software development. Programming the first instance of a database product costs a great deal, but almost nothing to make thousands of copies. So, if sales are high enough to pay for the upfront investment, each sale after that results in higher and higher profit margins.

Look for companies with greater than normal positive profit margins. Greater than 5% is good. Greater than 10% is better. Greater than 20% is excellent.

Finally, in the area of finance, Buffett believes a company should put its retained earnings to good use. If you look backward at what a company has done in previous years, you will see it has retained some portion of profits. Profits from business operations belong to the shareholders. In theory, the company could pay all of its profits out to shareholders. But that would leave it with nothing to invest in growth.

All companies choose to retain some profits to invest in growth. Check previous years' retained earnings to determine whether the money the company retained in 2007 resulted in higher shareholder equity in 2008. This is one way to measure whether the company is using the money well or is just hiding it in a bank account. If the company kept $5 million of profits in

2007, then it should be worth at least an additional $5 million in 2008. In actuality, if it has good uses for the money, it should have been able to generate additional profit on that money throughout the year. So if its profit margin is 10%, by 2008 that $5 million should have grown to $5.5 million in shareholder equity.

Comparing previous annual reports and online financial pages will show you what the company does with its money and whether it uses it to make the company better, bigger, and stronger.

Market Tenets

> What is the value of the business?
> Can the business be purchased at a significant discount
> to its value?

The final set of metrics determines how much the entire company would sell for if it were put on the market as a whole. Since each share is a fractional ownership of the whole, in theory, the sum of all of the shares represents the value of the entire company. If you multiply the individual share price times the number of shares outstanding, you get the market value of the company. For example:

$10 per share X 1 million shares outstanding
= $10 million in market capitalization.

In this example, $10 million is the price the market believes all the assets and earning power of the company is worth. But this price is driven by both an understanding of the company's position and the emotions of the buyers. Sometimes buyers are excited and may pay $20 per share for the company.

Has the company suddenly doubled in value? Has it somehow doubled its assets? Has the company doubled the profits it is able to generate? Has it shown some sign of doubling one of these in the near future? Usually, the answer to these questions is "no." The price jumps up because millions of investors have their own ideas about the company and are willing to pay more for it.

To escape this rollercoaster of market emotion, Buffett recommends calculating the hard value of the company as if it were being sold to a single investor in its entirety. How much would the company sell for? An investor would buy its assets, liabilities, reputation, and ability to make money. When all these are added up, they provide an idea of the value of the company in the same way that we all estimate the value of a product we buy in a store. Once this number is known, Buffett can determine when the stock price is low by comparison or whether it is too high. This allows him to buy companies when they are selling at prices close to their values if they were being sold as a single entity.

In some cases, a company's stock price drops so low its market value is actually less than the total cash it has in the bank. This means that if you could take out a loan to buy the whole company, you could use the cash in its bank accounts to pay off the entire loan. Then you would have everything else to do with as you please. You could sell the inventory and factories for a profit. Or you could keep it running to generate profits. Theoretically, this would be a bargain price for the company.

Another comparison of price to value is an analysis of the book value of the company. The book value reports the value of the company's assets minus its liabilities. You can compare the book value per share with the company's share price. When the share price you pay is near or even below the book value, it may be a very good deal. However, when the share price is much larger than the book value, even by a few multiples, a buyer would probably overpay for the company. Usually the share price of a well-run company with good future prospects is higher than its book value. But you should not buy shares of a company when you are paying more than two times book value.

These are some of Warren Buffett's key principles for buying stock in a company. You can see that collecting and understanding all this information requires some work, work that Buffett is willing to do, but that most people are not willing to do. As an individual investor, you can mimic Buffett's method and reap some degree of his success when choosing stocks to buy and when to buy them.

Jim Cramer, *Mad Money*

Judging by Jim Cramer's personality on his television show Mad Money, you might assume he is a wild and risky speculator. On the show, he jumps from one stock to another, dispensing advice and information about each like a rapid-fire machine gun. But, this is just what it takes to successfully run a call-in show like his and to keep viewers interested in a very dry and slow topic.

If you read his investing books, you will find Jim Cramer is very cautious, level headed, and focused on value investing in a manner similar to Warren Buffett. Or, at least that is the kind of advice he believes in giving to the general public.

Know Yourself

Cramer's first principle is not financial; it is personal. Know what kind of person you are. Do not make up a story about what kind of person you would like to be. Do not imagine what you will be like in a few years. Honestly assess what you are like right now. This seems trivial but it is essential if you are to have any control at all over your investment decisions.

Some people are genuinely "high rollers." They enjoy taking risks. They are thrilled by the possibility of big wins. They are not scared by big losses. Others are very conservative and cannot tolerate losing a single nickel. They cannot sleep if they are losing money and they are not happy if their investments are down, even temporarily. If you belong to the latter group, you really need to stick with more conservative investments. We all get out of our comfort zones occasionally, but we quickly make decisions to get back into the zone. If you are a conservative, risk-averse person, you will sell your stocks when they drop. Your temperament will force you to "sell low" just because you cannot stand the stress that the stock might decline further.

If you are more comfortable with risk, you might be able maintain your enthusiasm during declines and hold your stocks until things get better.

Knowing which of these styles is most like you will help you to choose investments that match this style, and will be investments you can live with day to day.

Confidence in your investments only comes with experience. If you are bothered you are far too conservative or far too risky then, as you learn more, you will gravitate toward a more balanced and unemotional approach to investing.

Do Your Homework

The most important step in becoming an experienced and successful investor is doing your homework. Cramer says repeatedly he does not believe in "buy and hold" for stocks. His philosophy is "buy and homework." He recommends you spend one hour each week studying companies, industries, and the market for each stock you own. Cramer believes there are good times and bad times to own a stock. The stock itself is not good or bad. Instead, there are good and bad times to be an owner. "Buy and homework" will lead you to see when it is a good time to get into a stock and when it is time to get out. Your homework will tell you the stock has run as high as it can go and it is time for a pullback. This is when you should get out and let the stock fall without you.

However, you will have to figure this out on your own. The financial press and your broker will not tell you when to get in and when to get out. The financial industry is biased toward being in the market at all times. They earn money when you are in, not when you are out. Second, most advisors tell their clients to get into a stock AFTER it has had a big run up. Once a stock has made a 20% gain you will see positive stories about it in the financial press. But where was that glowing recommendation before the stock rose by 20%? You will have to find that on your own.

What do you want to learn about a stock and the company when you are doing your homework? A few critical pieces of information that you need to learn are:
- How does the company make money?
- What sector is it in?
- How has it performed in the past?
- How does it compare with other companies?
- How does the balance sheet look?
- What is your decision?

So it looks like you have to read information about more than just the company you are interested in. You will have to understand a little about the whole industry. You will study the company you initially got interested in and then expand your knowledge to its competitors. What makes your company special? What does it have that every other company in the industry does not have? If it really has a special ingredient, can it hold onto it and keep other companies from copying it?

Everything you learn changes from month to month. This is why you need to keep doing your homework every week. You want to spot the changes before they are widely known to everyone in the market. You might not beat some of the big firms on Wall Street, but you can certainly beat all of the small investors who do not do any homework at all.

Control Your Trades

Jim Cramer also provides some excellent advice on how to execute your trades. You should be in control of the price you pay. Given an option between a market order and a limit order, you should choose to trade via the limit order. A market order will buy the shares at the next rate available from a seller. It is a guaranteed deal, but may cost you a little more to get the shares. However, the price of shares fluctuates all day long. Once you determine how much you want to pay for a share, enter a limit order requesting to buy or sell the shares only at the price you have decided on. This puts you in charge of the trade. If the stock does not trade at the price you specified, then the limit order prevents you from paying too much or getting too little.

Next, you should buy incrementally. If you want 1,000 shares of the company, you do not have to buy them all at once. You can by 250 or 500 now, and then look at the stock later in the day to see if you can get the remaining shares for a little less. This will prevent you from trading purely on your emotions. No one is so smart that we are always right. But we are all emotional. So breaking your trades into increments will pull at least some of your decisions out of your immediate emotional reaction.

When you buy stocks in the morning you usually trade with amateurs who spent the weekend reading and planning and are getting their trades done before becoming immersed in their jobs for the week. Monday morning is particularly heavy with amateur traders. This means the stock market tends to get an emotional boost in the mornings. That boost could be positive or negative. In the afternoons, the professionals regulate prices and stocks tend to move toward their more stable values. You can use this to your advantage when you know what the general sentiment is on a particular day or week.

When the mood is good, mornings are a good time to sell. When the mood is bad, mornings are a good time to buy.

Finally, Cramer suggests controlling your trades by selling your shares incrementally, just as you bought incrementally. When you have some really good gains that you want to lock in by selling, you should do it in multiple steps.

Don't Fight the Cycles
Some cycles in the markets are controlled by big mutual funds and hedge funds. These organizations trade millions of shares daily. When they decide to get into a stock, they will buy a lot of shares and cause its price to rise. If you know these guys are buying, you can buy in as well and enjoy the resulting price inflation.

More importantly, when a company turns in some bad profit numbers, restates past earnings, falls under an investigation, or has a major product failure, the big players will move out of the stock. You can rationalize all you want about how solid the company is. But when the big players sell major blocks of shares, the price will drop. If you want to capture your profits, you should sell with them. You can always come back into this company later, after the excitement is over. When you do this, you will get more shares for your money.

Stock prices are subject to gravity just like everything else in this world. That means it is easier for them to fall than it is for them to climb higher. It takes a lot of hard work, investment, and good management to grow a company and increase its stock price. But it takes just a few rumors or fear to cause the price to drop and lose the results of years of good work.

A decline in price of 25% cannot be made up by a subsequent 25% increase. Imagine a company is trading at $100 and then a rumor causes the price to drop $25 to $75 over a few weeks. For the price to rise from $75 to $100, it has to increase by $25. But this time, $25 is not 25% of the current price. Rather, it is 33% of $75. The company has to work a lot harder and produce more good news and higher profits to gain $25 than it did to lose $25.

Cramer says it is more important to avoid losing money than it is to make money. If you lose money, you have nothing to invest to get back in the game. But if you just avoid the loss, even at the expense of missing some gains, that is better than risking losing it all.

During the recent economic crisis, companies like Lehman Brothers and Merrill Lynch were both so focused on making quick profits they risked everything on credit default swaps. When this one investment class turned bad, these companies lost so much they completely collapsed and went out of business. In Lehman's case, the government let them fail and disappear. In Merrill's case, the government assisted in the sale of the company before it failed to Bank of America. Without this purchase, Merrill would have followed Lehman into bankruptcy.

Chapter 10

Mathematical Approaches

———————

The two authors discussed in this chapter are different from the investors discussed in Chapter 9. They advise more mathematical approaches to executing successful investment plans.

Phil Towne, *Rule #1 Investor*

Phil Towne is less of a successful investor and more of a successful investment book author. In *Rule #1 Investor*, Towne provides something missing in many of the above books. He gives specific numerical and mathematic guidelines for making investment decisions. Rather than just pointing to principles, he sets basic thresholds a company must achieve before it should be considered an investment.

Towne believes in looking back over the company's performance for at least five and preferably ten years. During such a length of time, the company should have faced most of the situations and challenges that await it in the future. You need to determine whether it has handled challenges successfully and profitably in the past. This is one of the best indicators you can get that it will be able to do so again in the future.

Performance Criteria

Towne believes a company should meet the following performance criteria over a ten-year period.

- Return on investor capital growing faster than 10% per year
- Shareholder equity growing faster than 10% per year
- Earnings per share growing faster than 10% per year
- Sales growing faster than 10% per year
- Cash growing faster than 10% per year

These are five simple criteria to understand. Most of this data are readily available on free financial Web sites like Yahoo! Finance or MSN Money Central.

When you find a company in which you would like to consider investing, you can collect the data in these areas and determine whether it meets all five criteria or just three or four. If it does, then perhaps it is a good and reliable company in which to invest over the long haul. If it does not meet most of these criteria, then Towne suggests it is too speculative. Continue looking for a solid performer.

Deciding a company is good is the first step in the process. The second step is determining the right price at which to purchase the company.

Purchase Price

Towne recommends a couple of basic formulas for attempting to estimate the future growth rate of a company, which suggests what it is worth today.

Future EPS

First, calculate the potential earnings per share for the stock ten years from now. This is necessarily a guess. It is impossible to know what twists and turns lie to be navigated by the company in the future. But, based on information available today, you can calculate a ten-year trajectory if things continue as they are now.

If you know the EPS over previous years, then you might project that it will continue along the same trend. Therefore, the EPS in ten years depends on the EPS today, scaled up by the growth rate of the EPS over the last few years.

Using mathematical notation, this can be written as:

$$EPS(10) = EPS(0) * (1 + EPS\ Growth\ Rate)^{10}$$

This says that the EPS in ten years, EPS(10), is equal to the EPS now, EPS(0), multiplied by ten years of growth at the EPS Growth Rate. All you need to complete the equation is the current EPS and the EPS Growth Rate from one of the financial Web sites.

A mathematician might be able to calculate this on paper or by using a calculator. But investors usually rely on a spreadsheet to do this work for them. You can enter this equation into a spreadsheet, or use the calculator Towne provides on the book's Web site.

Future Price to Earnings Ratio

The next number needed is an estimate of the price-to-earnings ratio (PE) of the company in ten years. Towne's research suggests that P/E is also a function of the EPS Growth Rate. He believes in ten years the P/E is twice the

EPS Growth Rate. Mathematically, the EPS Growth Rate is a percentage. This means that 3% is actually 0.03, so a spreadsheet needs to multiply the EPS Growth Rate of 3% by 100, meaning that it is actually just "3." Then you double it to come up with the P/E ten years from now.

The equation looks like this:

$$PE (10) = 2 * (100 * EPS\ Growth\ Rate)$$

Again, you can set this up yourself in a spreadsheet or use Towne's online forms.

Future Price

Using the future EPS and future P/E, you can now estimate the future price at which the stock will trade. In ten years, Towne's method estimates that a stock will trade at:

$$Price(10) = PE(10) * EPS(10)$$

Now, to create an example, assume that XYZ Inc. currently trades at $50 per share. It has an EPS of $2, which has been growing pretty consistently at 8% per year. Given this little bit of data, Towne estimates the trading price in ten years using the following simple formula.

$$EPS(10) = 2 * (1 + 0.08)\ 10 = \$4.32$$
$$PE (10) = 2 * (100 * 0.08) = 16$$
$$Price(10) = PE(10) * EPS(10) = \$69$$

If Towne's method is correct, in ten years you should be able to buy the stock now for $50 and sell it in ten years for $69. This is certainly a profit. But is it a good investment? That is the next calculation we will perform.

Everything in this equation is driven by three variables. The current price and the current EPS are known numbers. The EPS Growth Rate is also known based on prior years. The equations include one assumption about P/E - specifically that it is generally twice the EPS Growth Rate. The equations also assume the EPS grew at the same rate over the last 10 years it had grown during the previous three or four years. If both of these assumptions are true, then the equations will have good predictive power. However, if they are not true then the estimate will be far off the mark.

How do we assume the company will continue to grow as it has in the past? That is why we first looked at the company's historical numbers to determine whether the company was consistent over the previous ten years. If it was not consistent, then an estimate of future value based on consistent growth will not be appropriate.

No system can accurately measure the future. But the only hope a company might perform consistently in the future is evidence that it has done so in the past. If the company does not have a past record of consistent growth, this method of estimating its future cannot be true.

Knowing this, you should pay more attention to the first part of this exercise. When looking at the past, consistent growth is required before you can put any faith in the estimation method given here.

Time Value of Money

In the example, we believe the stock of XYZ Inc. will rise from $50 to $69. But money can be invested in a number of different ways. You should not invest in a risky asset like company stock rather than just putting the money in a Treasury bond or a certificate of deposit unless a high enough return exists to justify accepting the risk.

What rate should you demand from an investment to justify the risk? Investments in the stock market as a whole have tended to return 8% over the long term, not including dividends. (With dividends they have averaged between 10% and 11%.) But, you do not know which stocks performed above that and which below to arrive at an average of 8%. Therefore, when you are selecting an individual stock, you should look for one that you believe will return substantially more than 8%. Towne recommends looking for something at the 15% level.

So, if a stock has to return 15% per year to justify the risk, you have to calculate what the selling price would be today to meet that 15% level. The equation that does this is the following discounted cash flow equation:

$$\text{Buy-Price}(0) = \text{Price}(10) \, / \, (1 + rr)^{10}$$

In this equation, "rr" stands for the "rate of return" you want from your investments. Given the price you think the stock will reach in ten years, this equation will tell you what you should pay for it today to achieve the desired rate of return. Therefore,

$$\text{Buy-Price}(0) = 69 \, / \, (1 + 0.15)^{10} = \$17.06$$

Uh-oh! The equation says to achieve a 15% rate of return over ten years, you must buy the stock for only $17 today. Today's price of $50 indicates a poor investment if it will grow to just $69 in ten years.

In fact, using a little bit more math, you can calculate what the rate of return would be on an investment that grows from $50 to $69 in ten years.

$$Buy\text{-}Price(0) = Price(10) / (1 + rr)10$$
$$50 = 69 / (1 + rr)10$$
$$rr = 0.033 = 3.3\%$$

XYZ Inc. is a profitable investment. But given your estimate of its future value, it is only fractionally better than putting money into a CD. Since it is a much riskier investment that might lose money, you should not buy it at the current price. It is growing just too slowly to justify today's price.

Margin of Safety

Though we have eliminated XYZ as a candidate for investment, there is still one more step in calculating the price to pay for the stock today. Several decades ago, Benjamin Graham started preaching the "margin of safety" idea in selecting a stock. Even when the company seems to offer a very nice rate of return, you still have to account for the fact stocks are risky investments. Therefore, before buying, you should have a margin of safety in the price you pay. You should buy the stock when it is on sale, when the price is low enough that it is almost impossible to lose money on it.

Towne recommends a margin of safety be set at half of the Buy Price from the previous step. Therefore, he would buy XYZ Inc. at:

$$MOS\text{-}Price(0) = Max\text{-}Price(0) / 2$$
$$= \$17.06 / 2$$
$$= \$8.53$$

This is a pretty rough criterion for picking a stock. You can assume most of the companies you evaluate will not successfully pass the gauntlet of tests prescribed. Most companies are selling at least as high as the "Buy Price" and often much higher than that.

When the stock market is doing well and everyone is excited about his or her chances to make a lot of money, stock prices are inflated; they are too high. At those times, these tests will fail almost every company. This means it is a good time for you to have your money in cash. It is a good time to hold CDs and treasuries. You have already missed the buying opportunity. There may be just short-term gains to be had by speculators who get in and out before the bubble bursts.

But once the bubble of excited trading bursts, many stocks will go on sale. Many will then pass the tests prescribed by Towne. This is the time for you to purchase stocks. This is when there are bargains to be had. This is also when others are most fearful and their anxiety will affect you as well. Buffett says when others are fearful; it is time to be bold. Towne's steps will help you to make decisions when it comes time to be bold.

James Stewart, *Common Sense*

James Stewart the financial writer is a different person from James Stewart the actor. The writer tries to guide people into escaping their emotions when buying and selling stocks. His "Common Sense" formula for investing calls for each of us to be guided by one simple rule when trading stocks:

> Buy when the Index goes down 10%, sell when the Index goes up 25%

He wants people to ignore their panic and their euphoria. Recognize the stock market and individual stocks vary constantly, and the time to buy and sell should be driven by the numbers, not the emotions.

First, his buy/sell decisions are guided by one of the major indexes. It may be the Dow Jones Industrial Average (DJIA), Standard & Poor's 500 (SP500), or National Association of Security Dealers Quote (NASDAQ). You can choose to use any one of these as your thermometer for gauging whether it is time to buy or sell.

Stewart's Common Sense does not discuss the specific stocks you should trade. You will have to use some other method to find those, or you can buy and sell an index mutual fund rather than specific stocks.

When to Buy
To "buy low and sell high," you have to disconnect your decisions from emotions generated by the market. When the index drops 10%, your emotions will tell you to "sell, sell, sell." But that is exactly wrong. When the index is down 10% it is time to "buy, buy, buy." This will get you into a stock that is part of an index when the price is relatively low.

You want to buy stocks when others are selling them. You want to buy stocks when they are on sale. Since most of us waffle and worry about whether the market has fallen far enough to justify buying, Stewart gives us a concrete number at which to pull the trigger: When the index is down 10%, it is time to buy.

How much do you buy? Stewart recommends moving 10% of your available cash into a stock or an index when the index has fallen 10%. If the market falls 10% this week, you invest 10% of the money you have in cash. If it falls another 10% next month, you move another 10% into the market again. You keep doing this every time the market index falls, until you have reached the limit of the maximum amount you would ever want in the market.

This strategy will not get you into the market at the very bottom. This is an impossible feat that professionals accomplish only a few times in their lives, and then usually by accident. It will move you into the market in several steps, each capturing a current opportunity, but still leaving enough money to capture another if it happens.

When to Sell

Stewart recommends selling your stock when the index has gone up 25% from the point at which you bought the stock. Notice that you sell when the index is up, not when your particular issue is up. He is focusing on the state of the entire market, not on specific news on your company.

He recommends selling in the same size steps that you bought, 10% of your invested amount. When the market goes up 25%, you sell 10% of the money you have invested. If the market continues to climb, you will continue to sell in 10% increments.

Stewart's analysis of the history of the stock market indicates bull markets have an average appreciation of 50%. Bear markets have an average depreciation of 20%. His approach pulls profits out of the market when it is up by half the amount of the average bull market and invests when it is down by half the amount of the average bear market. He continues to buy and sell if the market takes another whole step in either direction, the Common Sense method will continue to capture profits as the market rises, and will capture valuable stocks as it falls.

Since most of us have full-time job and may not be able to monitor the stock market daily, this methods also allows us some flexibility when buying and selling. You might miss that exact 25% up point or 10% down point. But you can execute at 26% or at 11%, and the Common Sense method will still work for you.

Autopilot

If you really have faith in this method, you can set it on autopilot. You can enter buy and sell orders at specific levels. Your broker will then execute the buy or sell at a specific level regardless of where you are or what you are doing.

The formulaic method of buying and selling is specifically built to encourage this kind of automatic decision. Stewart is trying to get you to plan by the numbers, not by your emotions. Preloaded orders fit very well with his method.

Chapter 11

Intermediate Alternatives...
Three to Ten Years

Stocks trading on U.S markets are not the only investments you can use in the intermediate stage of your investing life. Even without getting extremely complicated, a number of other good investments are open to you. In fact, some of these investments will focus on other important decisions in your life.

International Stocks

As a consumer, you almost certainly buy and use goods from all over the world. Your clothing, food, carpets, appliances, and automobiles may come from a foreign company. You can choose to invest in these companies as well. If you do this, you should be aware of unique variables that will affect your investments and returns that do not occur when buying stocks on an American exchange.

First, many large companies are listed on the stock exchanges of multiple countries. You can buy Toyota stock on the New York Stock Exchange or on the Japanese Exchange. In New York, you buy in dollars through an American investment company. To buy stock in the same company in Japan, you could work through your American broker, but the order needs to be placed by a broker registered on the Japanese exchange. This will require paying additional fees to move the order through the system. It will also require converting your money into Japanese Yen to make the final purchase.

This makes no sense; your investment in Japan would have to go through more hands. It would take a little more time to execute. It would incur more fees. And it will be subject to foreign currency exchange rates. This is a lot of extra work and risk for a company that is also available as an American stock. Clearly, for a company like Toyota you would prefer to invest in the American stock to avoid the extra expenses and time.

However, if the company is listed only in a foreign country there are a few more issues. You might find it difficult to obtain information about the company in a language you understand. The company may be subject to a set of corporate laws and investment regulations with which you are unfamiliar. Accounting regulations in the foreign country may lead to terms different from those to which you are accustomed. Finally, some countries are not politically stable. Their stock markets may experience disruptions caused by political or social turmoil.

For all of these reasons and more, it is a good idea for an intermediate investor in the U.S to consider himself a novice investor when buying and selling foreign stocks.

Prepaid College Tuition

If you have children or are planning to have them, you should make plans for their education. Most states allow you to purchase tuition fees many years before your children are ready to go to college. These plans are structured just like the loans that you use to buy a car or a house. You make a down payment and then pay a fixed amount each month. The goal is to pay for your child's college expenses over a period of 10 to 18 years, rather than trying to cover it all during the years your child is in college. Prepaid College Tuition is a contract with the state education system to cover the cost of tuition and fees at a future date. Check with your specific state to get details about joining a Prepaid College Tuition plan.

Prices are generally lowest if you start when your child is born and pay a little each month over several years. In many cases, this investment will yield returns similar to the 15% we seek from stocks. However, putting money away for your child's education is a guaranteed investment. You cannot lose and are almost guaranteed a positive rate of return.

Because this is such a low risk with a high probability of need, prepaid college tuition is an excellent use of your money. If nothing else, it provides protection for your future earnings and investments. It insures these will not be drained dry by the need to pay tuition all at once when your children start college.

IRS 529 investment plans are different from Prepaid College Tuition. 529 plans are merely investments that can grow without paying taxes on the condition the money is applied to the child's college expenses. These plans are actually an investment in a package of mutual funds with a targeted date for withdrawal.

Bonds

Bonds are an alternative investment to stocks. You can purchase them through brokers directly from the governments or companies that issue them or as part of a mutual fund. Bonds are typically less risky than stocks but they are not without risk. The price of a bond fluctuates up or down just like a stock, beginning on the date it is issued and continuing until the date it is retired. During this time, many bonds trade among investors in the same way stocks trade. Most people who invest in a 30-year bond do not hold that bond to maturity thirty years from now. They purchase it either new at issue or from another investor. Then they hold it for a time to collect the interest that is paid. At some point, they may decide they do not want to hold the bond any longer and they sell it to someone else.

The price of the bond is different every time it is sold. The value to other investors changes constantly due to changes in the world economy. Because bonds carry a fixed rate of return, their attractiveness changes based on the returns available from other bonds that may have been issued at different times.

For example, when a bond is first issued, it may carry a rate of return of 5%. That was the prevailing rate when all the paperwork and registration was done to issue the bond. A $1,000 bond would originally sell for $1,000, or face value, because its rate of return is the same as you can get from other similar investments on the day it is issued. If you hold that bond for one year you will collect the 5% interest, earning you $50 on the bond.

But if new bonds are now being issued with a rate of 6%, no buyer will want to own your bond that pays just 5%. To make your bond attractive to a buyer, it must be sold below its face value. How much lower depends on the difference between the rate of your bond and the rate of new bonds.

If the new rate of return on a $1,000 bond is 6%, then an investor makes $60 per year on that bond. But your bond only returns $50. You have to lower the price you sell your bond for by at least $10 to balance out the values of the two bonds. Since the buyer may be planning to hold the bond for several years, he will see that he is getting a $10 discount on your bond and a $50 return the first year, which matches the $60 he can earn on a new bond. That's fine for one year but during the second year he will still earn $50 instead of $60. He will need a bigger discount than $10 to find your bond attractive. This is to make up for the $10 difference during subsequent years. In theory, the bond's selling price might have to be adjusted each year from now until it matures.

The concept of why it is discounted is easy to understand. Why it has to be discounted for the second, third, and subsequent years is also easy to understand. The mathematics of how much it has to be discounted to be on par with the 6% bond is a little more complicated. Most people rely on online calculators rather than working the formula themselves. A yield to maturity calculator will show you that to compensate for a change in interest rates from 5% to 6% over nine years remaining on a bond requires the price of the bond drop to $833. This is probably more of a drop than you might expect.

We will not go into the mathematics of this discount. What is important for you to realize is that if you are buying and selling bonds, the price you can get fluctuates based on the current interest rate and the original rate attached to your bond. This means a bond has many of the characteristics of a stock. When interest rates rise, the price at which you can sell your old bond declines. But when interest rates fall, other buyers find your old 5% bond to be more attractive than the new 4% bonds. They will then pay you more than the $1,000 face value of your bond.

An alternative exists to buying and selling bonds. You could hold the bond until maturity. If you do that, you will get back your initial purchase price of $1,000. If you buy a 10-year bond and hold it for 10 years, you know exactly how much you will earn in interest and how much will be returned to you at the end. As an individual investor, you can choose to buy and sell your bond, or to buy and hold it to maturity.

You can also use a bond mutual fund to invest in the bond market. These constantly buy and sell new and old bonds in their portfolio. They try to maximize the amount they earn. Hopefully, their actions will give you a higher return than you could get from buying your own individual bonds. Managers of these funds understand all the variables that affect the prices and returns of bonds and use that knowledge to get you a better return than you can get on your own – at least that is the theory.

There is another advantage to investing in bonds via a mutual fund. Since your money becomes part of a large pool that buys thousands of bonds, your risk is spread out. When you buy a single bond from a company, that company might go bankrupt and erase some or all of your investment in the bond. This is a risk you have taken in buying the bond. But when you invest in a bond mutual fund, the failure of any one company or bond issue will not wipe out your entire investment. Instead, it will have a small negative effect on the return of the entire portfolio.

A further wrinkle is that a bond's published yield to maturity assumes you reinvest interest at the same rate of return as the original bond. Twenty-five dollars every six months from your 5% bond is impossible to invest in a new bond, let alone the fact that getting the same rate of return each time is impossibility. Bonds are issued in minimum amounts of $1,000. The advantage of a bond mutual fund is that the manager can take your $25 and those of all the other investors, pool them, and easily have sufficient to buy more $1,000 bonds. Just pay attention to the fees charged by any fund you consider.

Now the basic methods and risks inherent in investing in bonds are clear to you. Bonds can be extremely stable, long-term investments. Or they can be assets that you buy and sell to make a profit, similar to stocks.

Bond Issuers

Who sells bonds to the public? Sellers can be any entity that needs to raise money today and who will pay it back over subsequent years. This includes the federal government, state governments, county governments, corporations, non-profit organizations, churches, and many more. When you look at all the bonds available for sale, you see a list of organizations that want to borrow money from you to run their operations or perhaps to build something. They all promise to pay interest while they use your money and return your principle investment at the end of the bond's term.

Bond rates vary based on the bond issuer. The U.S federal government is considered one of the safest issuers of bonds. There is almost no chance it will go out of business, so you are almost certain to receive your interest and return of your principle if you hold it to maturity. Every other organization is measured based on this standard of security. A state bond may offer a little higher interest rate and a county government still a little higher. Some states and counties have defaulted on their debt in the past. As a result, investors expect more interest from these borrowers to compensate for this added risk. Similarly, many companies have defaulted on their debts. They must pay even higher rates to attract buyers for their bonds.

Since any organization can offer bonds, you might find one offered by a medium-sized company you have never heard of. Such companies will typically offer higher yields than government bonds because they need to attract your attention and convince you to take a little more risk when lending them money.

Credit Rating

How can you determine which organizations are the safest and which are the riskiest?

Comparing interest rates is one obvious way of estimating credit risk. A company does not offer higher rates out of the goodness of its heart. It offers higher rates only because it needs investors to take a chance with their bonds rather than putting all their money into federal Treasury bonds.

That still does not tell you how much added risk exists compared with the federal government. It also does not tell you the difference for a company, non-profit, or church bond. To help you measure this, several rating agencies assign a score to the creditworthiness of every organization. Since a bond is a loan from you to that organization, its credit rating is exactly what you need to know before you lend them money.

Three of the largest and most widely recognized rating agencies are Moody's, Standard & Poor's, and Fitch's. Each of these has a unique rating scheme that is a variation on the grades assigned in school. These grades run from A through D. Moody's best rating is "Aaa." Standard & Poor's best is "AAA." Fitch's best is also "AAA." These are uniformly called triple-A ratings. Few companies maintain this highest level of credit. Presently there are just 20 such companies.

The ratings move down the scale from triple-A to B, C, and D as shown in the table.

Table 11-1. Bond Credit Ratings

Moody's		S&P		Fitch		
Long Term	Short Term	Long Term	Short Term	Long Term	Short Term	
Aaa		AAA		AAA		Prime
Aa1		AA+		AA+		
Aa2		AA	A-1+	AA	A1+	High grade
Aa3	P-1	AA-		AA-		
A1		A+		A+		
A2		A	A-1	A	A1	Upper medium grade
A3	P-2	A-		A-		
Baa1		BBB+	A-2	BBB+	A2	
Baa2	P-3	BBB		BBB		Lower medium grade
Baa3		BBB-	A-3	BBB-	A3	
Ba1		BB+		BB+		
Ba2		BB		BB		Non Investment grade speculative
Ba3		BB-		BB-		
B1		B+	B	B+	B	
B2		B		B		Highly Speculative
B3		B-		B-		
Caa1	Not Prime	CCC+				Substantial risks
Caa2		CCC		CCC		Extremely speculative
Caa3		CCC-	C	CCC	C	In default with little
Ca		CC				prospect for recovery
/				DDD		
/		D	/	DD	/	In default
/				D		

The competition for credibility among the three rating agencies works to keep them honest. If one were to favor certain bond issuers rather than providing an honest assessment for buyers, buyers may turn their attention and their trust to the competitors who appear to serve the needs of the buyer more faithfully.

Risk Pyramid

Many writers have represented the risk of bonds using a pyramid such as the one below. The bonds at the bottom are considered the safest and those at the top are the riskiest. In general novice investors should stick to bonds at the bottom. Intermediate investors can move into bonds from stable, established governments other than the United States. Advanced investors can invest in bonds starting with mortgage-backed securities and higher on the pyramid.

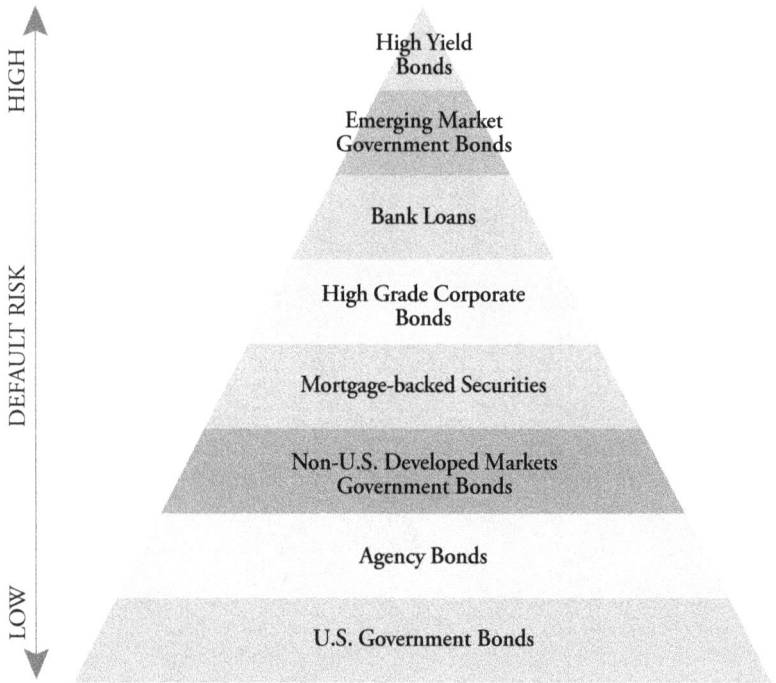

HIGH

DEFAULT RISK

LOW

High Yield Bonds

Emerging Market Government Bonds

Bank Loans

High Grade Corporate Bonds

Mortgage-backed Securities

Non-U.S. Developed Markets Government Bonds

Agency Bonds

U.S. Government Bonds

Figure 11-1. Bond Investment Pyramid

Calculating Bond Prices

The price of a bond is determined by using a number of complicated equations but the core variables that drive its price are:

- Bond rate of return
- Interest rate on new bonds
- Time to maturity
- Credit rating of the issuing organization

Jason Zweig, writer for the *Wall Street Journal* and other financial publications, recommends investors use bonds to earn interest with minimal risk. He warns against looking for those offering the highest returns. In all cases, these returns are a measure of the additional risk posed by the company issuing the bonds. He advises investors to choose a bond generating a typical or average return compared with other bonds or bond funds.

Real Estate

Another prime investment is real estate. During the right period and at the right point in the price cycle of real estate, you can become a millionaire using this investment. However, investing at the wrong time can lead to catastrophe. You must understand the cycle of prices that move the real estate market. It has repeated booms and busts. During the booms millionaires are minted all over the world. But during the busts millionaire are destroyed all over the world.

Most people move into real estate in four steps:
1) Buy their own home
2) Buy rental property
3) Buy multiple rental properties
4) Become a developer

Each step requires the investment of both more money and more time. Eventually, you will find yourself being a real estate developer or landlord full time. If you find the details and challenges of real estate interesting and rewarding, this may be the perfect investment track for you.

Buying vs. Renting

The argument about buying versus renting the house you live in is old. Most people have heard both sides of it many times over. It is a personal decision that has more variables than just the money involved. I believe people choose to buy or rent as a result of their lifestyles, rather than because of the financial implications.

In the U.S, home ownership is considered part of a successful life. In many European countries the majority of the population rents or leases their home for their entire life.

U.S tax law provides incentives toward home ownership by allowing you to deduct home mortgage interest from your income before calculating the taxes you owe. This makes the interest on your mortgage effectively 25% to 38% less by recouping taxes that would have been paid on those dollars.

Mortgages are also the focus of dozens of schemes to achieve lower monthly payments or to pay off the loan quicker and to reduce its interest over the life of the loan. Two of my favorite and simplest schemes involve doubling up.

The first doubling scheme is to simply make half of your mortgage payment every two weeks, rather than making a single payment every month. Because part of the payment is applied to the principle two weeks early, the amount of the loan is slightly smaller. This means slightly less interest accumulates each month. If you have a 30-year mortgage and are religious about following this technique every month, you will find you can pay off your mortgage seven years early. Your 30-year mortgage will be gone in 23 years and you will not have paid a penny more to make it happen. You will just have paid many pennies two weeks earlier. This eliminates seven years worth of interest payments. It is a piece of financial magic you really cannot refuse to use.

The second doubling scheme requires getting an amortization schedule of your loan. This schedule will show the amount of each monthly payment is allocated to principle and the amount that is allocated to interest. You will be disturbed to see in the beginning almost every dollar is used to pay accumulated interest. Only a few dollars cover the principle. Using this schedule, you can move yourself ahead in your payments by adding just a little money to each payment you make. You can look at the few dollars due for principle next month and add those to your payment this month. When you do that, you have effectively moved yourself forward one month in the payment schedule. Also, you have avoided paying that one month's interest. Do this religiously from the very beginning of the loan and you will pay off the loan in 15 years. This scheme is very easy in the beginning, but becomes more difficult in later years when the monthly principle amount comprises 25% or 50% of the entire payment. At that point, you need to make a payment 50% larger than you are required to. When you see how small the payments toward principle are in the first few years, you should make two or three payments ahead of schedule. I used to try to pay as many months ahead as I could. By the end of the first year of the mortgage, I had moved my payments into the fourth or fifth years of the loan.

When you set out to buy your home or rental property, you need to read a couple of books dedicated to real estate investing and learn all of the tricks, tools, and practices that can save you thousands of dollars with just a little extra effort. Do not rely on your banker to help you avoid paying interest; that is the core profit of the bank.

Location, Location, Location

The key to the value of a home and the land it sits on is not how beautiful it is, but rather its location. If thousands of buyers want a home in the same area, the surrounding property will sell at a premium to a similar house in a remote location to which no one wants to move. You want a house that meets your needs and the needs of the next buyer. There are beautiful pieces of property in the mountains of Wyoming and Alaska, but unless a road leads to the land a normal, sane person has no reason to want to live there. Its price will remain low for decades.

My relatives were part of a rural boom in agriculture. They moved into small and growing towns spread throughout the Midwest. These towns emerged to serve the needs of farmers and ranchers spread across thousands of acres. Many became railroad stops where cattle and crops were loaded for transport to cities. These little boom towns all had a single school, post office, and general store. Some grew into larger county seats, but many remained small, with just one or two hundred citizens. When the processes for delivering cattle and crops to the market changed, the need for these towns disappeared. Today, hundreds of these little towns are scattered across the plains of America. Where a town might once have held 100 people, it may now hold only ten or twenty. Many of the homes stand empty for decades because there is simply no one who is interested in owning them or living in them.

This same shift in interest happens to large cities. Detroit and the towns dedicated to the American auto industry have been emptying for decades. Today, entire subdivisions are practically empty. Homes in Detroit are sometimes put up for auction and draw no bidders even at a price of $500.

When you choose the location you want to own property, try to find a place your next buyer will like as well. That is the only way the property will hold its value or appreciate.

Leverage Equity

When real estate prices climb higher and higher, you can use a number of tricks to get a bigger piece of this pie. But understand that these tricks always involve additional risk. When prices are rising, it is easy to let excitement convince you these tricks are a "sure thing." It seems as if there is no way you can lose on the deal.

In truth, there are thousands of people who thought exactly the same thing during the last real estate boom and held too much leverage for too long. Many were wiped out and driven into bankruptcy when the boom ended. Never be deceived into believing you are too smart to be caught like they were. Always realize, among the millions of other people investing to make money, at least thousands of them are smarter than you.

Here is a favorite trick that worked in the last real estate boom. Buy a rental property and put 10% down. Rent it out for enough to make the payments every month. If you bought a $100,000 house, you have only $10,000 invested in the property. If you wait for five years, that house may appreciate to $150,000. The $50,000 is appreciated value to you that you did not have to pay for in cash. You earned it through wise selection of the property and the effects of time.

You can now borrow an additional $50,000 against it and add that amount to the mortgage. Then you can use that $50,000 to buy a bigger property. You might buy a $500,000 house and use the entire $50,000 for a down payment. If you wait another five years, you may find that your first house has appreciated by another $50,000. Your second house may have appreciated by $250,000, which adds up to $300,000 in equity you can take out of these properties and use as a down payment for a third property.

If the real estate boom continues long enough, you can do this repeatedly. Within 20 years, you will be able to easily take out $1 million worth of accumulated equity. However, when the boom stops, the game will be over and the series of houses you bought will have to be self-sustaining. If the housing market drops, the value of your homes could fall below the amount you owe on them. In theory this does not matter as long as the renters continue to make the rent payments you set up for them. But if they are tempted to move away or demand a reduction in monthly rent, you will have to find a source of money to make the payments that are no longer covered by your renters.

This is how some real estate investors get caught in a trap. They were deep in the heart of this scheme, or another like it, when the real estate bubble burst and their properties became worth less than they owed in loans. Be careful. Be conservative. Have a buffer between investing and the poor house.

Collectibles

Collecting antiques, art, comic books, old cars, and Beanie Babies is also considered an investment activity. But really, for most people such activity started as a personal hobby which just happened to turn into a good investment. My aunt collected ceramic owls of every shape and size. She had cookies jars, salt shakers, spoon rests, desk clocks, wall clocks, picture frames, and dozens of knick knacks that were decorative owls. Although she was investing in ceramic owls, the price appreciation meant nothing to her since all she wanted was owls in every corner of her house. The owls appreciated in price as they became pieces of nostalgia and rare items to other owl collectors. She never sold any of them, but in theory had thousands of dollars worth of these collectibles.

For most people, collectibles are items that provide inner pleasure in owning them. It is an added benefit that their price also appreciates. The collections might have a price tag, but they are unlikely to be sold to pay college tuition or to make a down payment on a home.

In 1983, I had a 1972 yellow Ford Mustang Mach I. It was a beautiful car that was a joy to drive. My father paid $2,000 for it. In 2010, I saw a similar car at a dealer in Iowa. It was priced at $18,500. A quick calculation shows the potential appreciation in value of my yellow car might have been 7.7% per year over those 27 years, or 823% over thirty years. That is a pretty good return, even better if you can assume there was little risk that a 1972 Mustang would ever depreciate in value.

When you combine that appreciation with the enjoyment that I could have had in owning and driving the car, the value is both financial and personal. But if you begin to deduct the cost of maintaining the car, much of the financial appreciation disappears. Keeping the car would require paying taxes, insurance, gasoline, maintenance, and storage. If I had been actively driving the car, I could also have experienced an accident. It could have been carried away by a tornado when I lived in Texas or smashed in a hurricane while I was in Florida.

These kinds of expenses are one of the primary reasons people prefer to invest in intangibles like stocks and bonds. You can own a fraction of a car company with far lower overhead than you can own an entire car.

When I was in high school, I met a woman with a superb collection of comic books she was trying to sell. I had a job and had saved quite a bit for a kid. Looking through her collection, I picked out a few comics that really appealed to me. Even then I thought these would appreciate in price. I pulled *Iron Man #1* and *#2, Submariner #1*, and a few others from her collection. When it came time to hand over the comics, she pulled back *Iron Man #1* but let me have #2. I paid her $2 for that comic book. I have read it several times and kept it bagged and stored for over 20 years. Today, it might sell for $75—an annual return of 12.8%, or a thirty-year return of 3,649%. It was a great investment. But, like a Mustang, the comic book requires storage and maintenance. As great as this investment was, the hitch is that I could not find one thousand of these comics to invest in. Only one was available. So, I have a great investment in storage that is worth $75. I will never sell it. I will keep it and pass it on to my grandchildren.

You might be surprised to learn that *Submariner #1* was a much better investment than *Iron Man #2*. I also paid $2 for Submariner and today it sells for $125, a 14.8% annual return or a thirty-year return of 6,135%.

I bought these collectibles when they were obviously going to be valuable in the future but before they had become really rare or really popular. At that point, how was I to know $2 for a comic book or $2,000 for a car was a fair price? If you are going to buy collectibles as investments, you need to put in the time to research the items in which you are interested, just as you would for a stock. But this research will enlighten you on the value of an asset that you can only buy one at a time. You need to find a lot of *Submariner #1* comic books to create an entire investment portfolio.

This is why many collectors prefer to focus on artwork that sells for between $2,000 and $200,000. With art, you can research and buy just a few items and have an investment large enough to make a difference in your wealth. Art is also a lot easier to store than an automobile but has its own challenges in terms of maintenance and insurance. It is a lot more fragile than a Mustang and needs to be kept away from humidity, direct sunlight, pets, and small children.

All collectibles are unique items that require a unique buyer. It takes more time to find someone who will pay the price you want for these investments. Given the limitations, you can see why collectibles really are driven by someone's personal desire and pleasure in owning the item. Most real investments have shifted to abstract holdings like stocks and bonds because it costs almost nothing to maintain them over decades, there are millions of them available, and the market for them is very large.

Chapter 12

Experienced Investing...
Over 10 Years

W hile you maintain a daily job, investing will be your second profession. Your trading will be limited by your ability to remain current on world politics and the economy. You will also have a limited amount of time to participate in the market. There will be days and weeks when you will not have the time to look for trading opportunities. This is the primary reason I place the level of "experienced investor" at ten years. Certainly, the young MBAs on Wall Street become experienced much faster than that. If you have a full-time job separate from investing, it will take you longer to reach that level.

It is not necessary that you ever reach the experience levels we discuss below. You can become a millionaire employee using just the beginner and intermediate investment vehicles we have already talked about. But many will master those investments and be eager to move on to more advanced vehicles.

In this chapter, we will introduce you to options, municipal bonds, and commercial real estate. We will not discuss short selling. In my opinion, shorting stocks is not appropriate for part-time investors trying to leverage income from their profession into a million dollars. Short selling is for professional investors with time to fully understand their positions and who can afford to take big losses. The Millionaire Employee can accomplish something similar to short selling using put options, and with much less risk.

Options

All financial instruments evolved from a need by businesses to support the financial needs of their ordinary operations. In some cases, the needs of the business are directly tied to a specific financial instrument, like loans and bank deposit accounts. In others, the financial instrument was not needed until the business became more complex, more profitable, and more expensive. Stocks and bonds were created to support much larger operations than could typically be financed with simple bank loans.

Options go a little further. They allow businesses to buy and sell goods or capture financing based on future expectations. Options evolved from commodities trading. Farmers needed money to purchase seed, fertilizer, and equipment to plant crops. Rather than taking out a loan, a farmer sold his crop before it was even planted. He gave a financier the option to take possession of his crops at a specified price. Both parties had to estimate the future value of that crop and both had to compromise a little to arrive at a price that was beneficial to both. In the end, the financier typically sold his rights to the crop to a mill that could actually turn wheat into flour. But by serving as a middle man, the financier helped the farmer with immediate cash and even gave the mill owner the opportunity to look for a bargain on wheat as the expected price changed from day to day or week to week before it was harvested and delivered.

If options can work for commodities like farm products, they can also work for other financial instruments, so they have been applied to essentially all investment products. In this chapter, we primarily talk about stock options because of their liquidity and the efficient markets that exist for any investor to trade them.

An option is a contract between a buyer and a seller to exchange an asset such as a stock at a given price any time during the period of the contract. Both sides have different expectations about what will happen to the price of that stock during the period of the contract. One party to the contract is guessing the price will rise, while the other expects it will not rise. Or, one side expects the price to decline, while the other expects it will not decline. In both cases, it is important to realize that, as sure as you are about your expectations, another person is just as sure of the opposite.

This is important because it implies an equal number of optimistic and pessimistic investors. No one investor is ever right all of the time, including you.

The price of an option reflects the current price of the stock, the agreed upon exchange price in a contract, the accumulated opinion of the market on that stock, and the number of days remaining until the end of the contract.

Stock options are settled once a month on the third Friday of the month. This means all option contracts run from the day they are purchased to the third Friday of a particular month in the future. You can buy a contract that runs through the current month, two months, or longer. Because time and market conditions change constantly, the price of an option also changes constantly.

Assume that all financial and psychological variables are held constant. Market conditions will be the same on the second of the month as they were be on the first. Even when this happens, the price of the option for the same stock should drop slightly because the time left on the contract is one day shorter.

Option prices change constantly for all the reasons that underlying stock prices change from minute to minute. Option prices also change because they are a contract with a fixed date of maturity. When that contract ends, you must decide to either pay for the stock at the agreed upon price or let the option expire unexercised.

The financier who makes a loan to the farmer to buy seed does not want to take ownership of the wheat. His role is just to serve as a middle man to help bridge the time between when the farmer buys seed and when he can sell his crops. The financier plans to sell ownership of the wheat to a mill before the wheat is put on a truck and delivered. The mill is really the only participant with the means to receive and store the wheat once it is harvested.

Similarly, you might never want to take ownership of a stock. Instead, your role may be in trading through the month, but before the contract ends you decide to sell it to another investor who really does want to own the stock. During the life of the contract you have the ability to sell it to someone else. Options markets make it possible to buy or sell an option on any trading day or hour regardless of when the contract ends.

Farm Auctions

My Uncle George loves to attend farm auctions. He goes with a pocket full of cash and looks for bargains for someone who can use them. His primary focus has always been automobiles and Indian arrowheads. He attends dozens of auctions every year and knows how to price his purchases. He might look for a car to keep for a few years. Or, he might look for a bargain to sell at a profit. The resale might happen in a few days or months. It might also happen that same day at the same auction.

George may see a car selling for less than it should and he will aggressively pursue it up to a certain price. If he succeeds, he has the opportunity to resell it at a profit. Maybe the car will need some repairs to improve its value or maybe it is ready to resell right now.

Occasionally, he is the highest bidder, but before he even leaves the auction another buyer will approach and offer to buy the car from him at a higher price. This person might have been late arriving and missed the auction. He might have been unwilling to jump into the auctioning process. Or more likely, he saw George was the only serious bidder and decided to let him purchase it at a low price specifically so that he could make an offer directly to him rather than driving up the price in the public auction. Uncle George may resell the vehicle before he even takes possession of it and in some cases before he makes payment.

This is very similar to selling an option on a stock before the contract expires. George's goal was to make a profit on the asset, not necessarily to take possession of the asset.

My 88-year-old uncle has never bought stocks or options, but through his trading at farm auctions he understands the concept behind both. His expertise is in used automobiles and obscure Indian arrowheads rather than in the more abstract shares of publicly traded companies.

Call Option
Early models of the atom suggested it was composed simply of protons, neutrons, and electrons. Everything in the universe was believed to be formed

by these three subatomic particles. The options market is similar in that it is made up of two basic instruments, the call and the put. But just as scientific advances showed that the atom had many more components than the basic three, call and put options can be used in dozens of different combinations to fit different situations. In this book we will just introduce the basic call and put options, you can see more in-depth discussions about options in other books that we recommend.

The "call" is an offer from a buyer to purchase a stock at a specific price within the next few months. In exchange for the right to make the purchase at the specified price, he is willing to pay a fee, which is the price of the option. The size of the fee depends on many variables. The most important of these are the current price of the stock, the price he is contracting to buy the stock for in the future, the number of days left in the contract, and market expectations as expressed in the number of people willing to sell such a contract to him.

Let's use an example. Suppose that XYZ Inc. is currently trading at $22 a share. A very conservative buyer might just want to lock in the right to buy the stock at $22 next month. Someone else might be happy to sell his or her XYZ stock in the next month at a price of $22. To be persuaded to wait for the deal to close, the current owner of the stock will want to be paid a small fee. In fact, many people may be willing to sell the buyer the right to call their shares at $22, but each may want a different price for that right. One seller might want $0.55 a share, another $0.65, and a third $0.75. The options market will match the buyer with a seller to fill the call order with as many as he wants at a specified price, or with as many that the sellers are willing to offer at his price. He might get a contract for 100 shares from the first seller at $0.55. The next 100 shares might come from the second seller at $0.65. In this case, to purchase contracts for 200 shares of XYZ the buyer would have to pay:

$$\$0.55 \text{ X } 100 + \$0.65 \text{ X } 100 = \$120$$

He does not buy 200 shares of stock at $22 for $4,400 today. Instead, he spends only $120 for the right to buy those shares at $22 anytime between now and the end of the next options period.

Why would a buyer do this? He is effectively paying a $120 premium over the current stock price to just buy the stock. It's because he hopes the stock price increases before his options expire. If it does, he could buy the 200 shares at just $22 per share, or $4,400 for all of them, plus the call contract price of $120. If the price has gone up to $23, he will have an instant profit of $1 per share minus the $120 price of the call contract. This is not as good as having the entire $200 in profit. But he only spent $120 to earn $200. If he had bought the stock outright, he would have risked $4,400 to earn $200.

In this case, the option returned a 67% profit in just one month. The option buyer spent $120 and received back $200, or $80 in profit. $80 is 67% of $120. The same stock purchase would have yielded only a 4.5% profit. He would have spent $4,400 to buy the stock and would have earned $200 in profit.

If XYZ had declined in value to $21, then option buyer is not required to purchase the stock. He could simply let the seller keep the $120 and do nothing. He is out $120. But since he did not buy the stock and its price dropped, he limited his losses. His risk is limited to $120.

The seller of the call was betting the stock's price would not increase before the end of the contract. He was expecting to make $120, and at the end of the contract to continue holding the stock. If the stock price did increase, the seller would have been forced to sell his shares at $22, making $4,400 plus the $120 on the call option.

Call options are often diagramed as shown in Figure 12-1. The horizontal axis is the selling price of the stock when the option expires. The vertical axis shows how much profit or loss is made on that date.

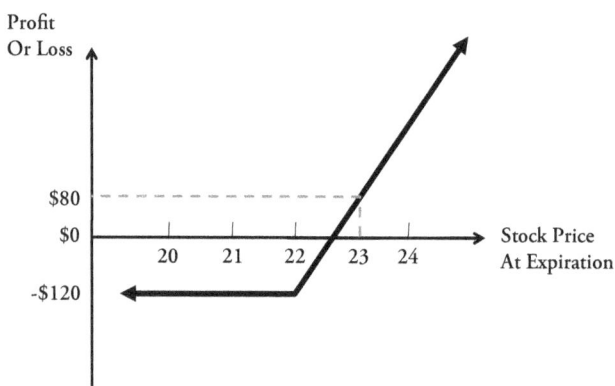

Figure 12-1. Call Options Profit Graph

Both sides of the transaction believe something different about the price of the stock and both are willing to place real money on their beliefs. There is no way to know which one is right until the market moves during the days of the contract.

For the options market to work, someone has to believe the exact opposite of what you believe and to be so certain in this belief they are willing to put their money on their opinion. In the example, you could just as well have been the person selling the option because you believed that the stock price would not increase in the next few weeks.

With a call option, the buyer pays for the right to buy a stock at a specific price before the contract expires. The seller receives a payment in return for accepting the obligation to deliver the stock at the given price if the buyer wants it. So, when the call is created, the buyer pays to have a little power and the seller receives money in exchange for giving up a little control over their stock.

Put Option

The mechanics of the put option are exactly the same as a call option except the buyer of a put pays for the right to sell stock at a given price during the life of the contract. He does this because he believes the stock price will decline during that time and he will hold a contract allowing him to sell at a price above where it might be near the end of the contract period.

Conversely, the party selling the put receives money and in exchange is obligated to purchase the stock at the put price if the buyer wants to execute the contract. The seller bets the stock price will not decline but will remain at or above its current price through the end of the contract period.

The typical graph showing the outcome of a put option is similar to that of a call, but with the profit line flipped around (Figure 12-2). The buyer of the put makes more money if the price goes down and less if it goes up.

We will use the exact same prices as in the call option above to illustrate the put. The buyer wants to purchase a put option with the right to sell the shares in a month at a price of $22. He is betting that the price of the stock is going down. He purchases 100 puts at $0.55 each and another 100 from a second seller at $0.65. Therefore, he pays $120 for the right to sell XYZ stock at a price of $22 within the next month.

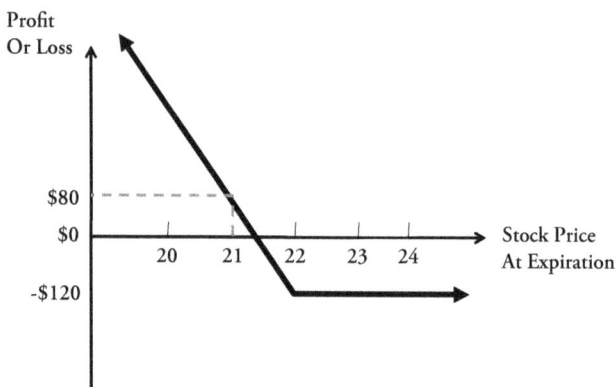

Figure 12-2. Put Option Profit Graph

The sellers earn $120 from this deal, but they have entered into a contract to sell their shares at $22 if the buyer requests it. If the price of the stock falls to $21 per share, then the option buyer earns $200. Since he paid $120 for the put contracts, his profit on the deal is $80.

However, at the end of the month, if the stock price is still at $22 or has risen higher, then his options are worthless. He has lost his $120 bet and the sellers have made the profit from the deal.

Options Strategies

If you believe a stock is fairly priced and will not move appreciably up or down in the next month or two, you might choose to sell both a put and a call to make a little extra money. If you are right, you will not have to buy shares as a result of the put or sell any as a result of the call. If you are wrong, you might be forces to sell shares at a price below the current market price. Or, you might find yourself buying shares at a price above what is available on the market.

This is just one example of dozens in which you can combine a put and a call to bet on something very specific. The professional traders on Wall Street have worked out a set of trades that will make money under every conceivable future behavior of the market. The trick is in knowing what will happen in the future so that you or they select the right strategy today which will make a profit in the future. If you select the wrong strategy you will lose money.

Those are the basics of options markets. There are a number of unique combinations which are too complicated to describe here.

When you are ready to learn more, I recommend that you dig into a couple of well-written and well-organized resources, such as:
- *Winning with Options: The Smart Way to Manage Portfolio Risk and Maximize Profit*, by Michael Thomsett.
- *Options and Options Trading: A Simplified Course That Takes You from Coin Tosses to Black-Scholes,* by Robert Ward
- Chicago Board of Options Exchange, Education Resources at **http://www.cboe.com/**

Thomsett's book does an excellent job of explaining the intricacies of options trading in terms that are pretty easy to understand. I used it to get started and representatives at my brokerage company told me that during my very first trade I knew more about options than most of their customers ever learned. Ward's book goes into much more detail on a large number of combinations. It is definitely for a more experienced options trader.

The Chicago Board of Options Exchange (CBOE) has put a great deal of effort into creating really useful online courses about options. You can take a number of the courses for free. They also provide an options calculator which is loaded with excellent lessons of its own.

You should take as many of the CBOE courses as you can. Then download the calculator, install it on your computer, and work your way through the lessons embedded in it.

This introduction to options is just to familiarize you with the major concepts involved in trading. It is no substitute for the two books by Thomsett and Ward or the CBOE courses. Before you start trading, you must learn all that these have to offer.

Tax-Free Bonds

There is nothing particularly complicated about tax-free bonds. They are just bonds issued by a government organization and they pay interest that is not taxable. All kinds of governments take advantage of this to pay a lower rate of return in exchange for the benefit to you of not being taxable.

Tax-free bonds are sold by national, state, county, and city governments. Your city might issue bonds to raise money for a new community swimming pool. The bonds will bring in a few million dollars to pay for the work right now. But the city can then pay the interest on the bonds for a few years and collect enough money over several years to pay off the principal.

Tax-free bonds are used to finance all kinds of government projects, including roads, water treatment plants, and buildings. Like other bonds, they carry the risk that the issuer will default. The U.S government has always been regarded as a "risk free" issuer. Though it is not actually without some risk, it is one of the lowest risks that exist. State, county, and city governments are all considered more risky than the federal government.

Tax-free bonds are listed in the experienced investor chapter because they are chosen over corporate bonds primarily for their tax advantage. This advantage is generally not significant unless you are in a 38% tax bracket or higher. If you are in a lower tax bracket, you can usually get a corporate bond that pays 15% or 25% higher interest to make up for the taxes you have to pay.

Professional Investing

Experienced investors often become professional investors because they earn more money through their investing activities than from other employment. This should be expected. Investment brokers on Wall Street step right into six-figure jobs and soon find themselves making millions every year. As a part-time but diligent professional, you should be able to reach the $100,000 to $1 million level as well.

When this happens, you will be far beyond the advice provided in this book and will have learned 100 times more than you can find here. This book will have been just one stone in the foundation of your own mansion of wealth.

Chapter 13

Winning and Losing

Because you are smart and well educated, you will be the first person in history to make only good investments. Everything you put your money into will increase in value. And, this trend will start on the very day you make your first investment. Your investment will politely continue to increase in value until the day after you sell it. Once you are no longer invested in it, it will decline in value, specifically to show you that you are smart and make only the very best decisions.

This is the fantasy many investors hold in their heads. They believe they somehow have the power to make only good decisions. Everyone believes she has super powers when it comes to investment decisions and she should be able to leverage that super power to make more money than everyone else because she never makes mistakes. It is not clear where this superior power comes from and what in her background or genetic makeup gives her this special insight others do not possess. But the less educated and experienced someone is, the more certain she seems to be that she has this super power.

Let me be the first to tell you that you do not have a super power for investing. You will not be the first person in history to make all of the right investments and avoid all of the wrong ones. Millionaires and billionaires who invest full-time still make mistakes. Even Warren Buffett does not have super powers in investing. He has made a number of costly mistakes during his investing career, and continues to make them today in his 80s.

Losing Money

You will make mistakes when investing. You will lose money on some investments. A few of these mistakes will be painfully and frighteningly large. This is normal. This is to be expected. This happens to everyone so you will not be alone.

Are you prepared to take some losses?

Can you live with making mistakes?

As an active investor, your objective is to make fewer mistakes than successes. If you have only three winners and seven losses in ten you can usually make money. As an active investor, you need to make sufficient profits to give yourself a good return over time despite losses. One advisor suggests the first thing you should learn about investing is how to take a loss, not how to make a profit. Take care of the losses and the profits take care of themselves.

With time, experience, and education, you will make fewer mistakes. But you will never entirely escape making mistakes. Every investor becomes rich because he or she makes better right decisions than wrong ones. In some cases, an investor's entire net worth is the result of one good decision that paid off so well it set him up for life. Warren Buffett had one of these good investments when he was young. He bought into GEICO Insurance at a time when everyone else thought little of the company. That single purchase put him into the ranks of the best long-term investors ever.

Buffett did not buy GEICO as a long-shot bet that *might* pay off. He analyzed its position and realized he had found an undervalued company that would do very well in the future. He aggressively bought into the company and used it as the basis for many of his future investments. You are looking for a similar opportunity.

As Buffett would say, *"When the odds are in your favor, bet heavily."* When Warren Buffett loses money, does he throw in the towel and quit as an investor?

Will you throw in the towel when you lose money? This is crucial for you to know early in your career.

Because loses can be painful, you need to take special joy in your successes. Do not take your successful investments for granted. You really need to enjoy them and celebrate them. You need to understand why they worked so well and look for ways to repeat them. The joy of your successes will give you strength against the agony of your mistakes. We all agonize over the mistakes we make. They are painful. We criticize ourselves for not being able to predict the future. Many people quit when they experience a loss. But that is the time to remember the joy of your successes and to look forward to making good investments in the future.

If you quit when you are down, you will exit the investment world. You will find few opportunities to help you to recover that money. You cannot recover from your losses by sitting on the sidelines. You must understand what caused your losses and do something to fix that problem.

Your losses may have been a result of a lack of knowledge. You may require more education in investments. The losses may have come from a flaw in your system of investing. You may need to adjust your strategy. If so, you might consult the strategies of the experts profiled in an earlier chapter. Your losses may have come from your own emotional reactions. You might have bought or sold at exactly the wrong time because you allowed your emotions to drive you rather than using good judgment and analysis. Fear and greed are horrendously dangerous to an investor. Finally, you may have experienced losses because of events beyond your ability to know or control. There are times when the market simply crashes and both professionals and amateurs are caught in the fall. When that happens, you cannot blame yourself. You just need to pick up and continue on from where you are.

This happened in May of 2010 when the Dow Jones Industrial Average fell 997 points with the speed of a runaway freight train. Even the professionals on the floor of the exchanges were unable to explain what happened.

There is another aspect to losses you need to be aware of. Losses carry with them the temptation to sell winners too early while there is profit to cover some of the previous losses. Fall prey to this temptation and not only will you still have the previous losses but you will also have fewer profits to make up for them.

If you remember James Stewart's Common Sense investing strategy, you will notice he sells a stock when it is up 25% and buys it when it is down 10%. Some portion of your portfolio is in the market when the market drops by 10%, meaning you will have lost 10% of your investment. But when your stock is up 25% and you sell, you capture 2 ½ times as much as you lost. Taken in aggregate, you have increased the invested portion of your investment portfolio by 15%. The 25% profit on a good move compensates for the 10% loss from a bad move. In practice, the gains and losses do not exactly balance out, but the example illustrates the point that a good strategy will make enough money to recoup your losses and give you a return better than you could have achieved had you not been invested.

Welcome to the world of investing your hard-earned money. You will earn more than your friends who keep their funds in a savings account. You will also experience the thrill of victory when you are right and the agony of defeat when you are wrong. As an investor, you buy into both these emotional extremes so be ready to both enjoy the highs and not let the lows discourage you.

Examine Yourself

The first steps in a successful investment career have nothing to do with investing money. They have to do with you. You need to examine *you* carefully before you examine stocks. How do you honestly and rationally believe you will react when you lose? How will you react when you lose almost every day for two or three years as happened twice in recent times in the first decade of this century? How do you think you will react if you not only lose day after day but also hear daily or hourly reports of how bad the economy is? This will happen to you.

If you have not already crossed this bridge in your mind you will do what many thousands of investors...no, *speculators*...did in August of 2008. They threw in the towel at the worst possible time in that terrible bear market. *This sort of thing happens in every bear market* to starry-eyed would-be millionaires who have not prepared themselves to face reality. These people, in an effort to preserve the value they still have, flee the market in droves at the very bottom. Instead of preserving capital, they preserve losses. This is what creates the final selling climax for which markets are well-known. It is what professional investors expect and wait for; buying at this time is how professional investors make much of their money.

It is not a conspiracy of the insiders against the lambs; it is simply a matter of professionals understanding what the vast masses of retail investors will do given that they have not prepared themselves mentally for the realities of the market.

Controlling the natural flight mechanism all endangered animals possess is difficult but it can be controlled more easily by preparing your mind with logic in calmer times. Panic tends to drive logic out the window so it needs to be applied in calmer times to reduce the likelihood of panic. If you feel you cannot do this, stay away from any kind of investment, resign yourself to not becoming a millionaire investor, but keep your sanity.

Recognize, too, you will most likely not get in at the very bottom of the market and out at the top. Smarter people than you have tried since the world's very first investment. Having recognized this, study loss probabilities. We have already said there will be times when you will lose. Okay, how much? A bear market is typically defined as a loss of 20%. Here are some historical bear market records. Read them carefully to see what they mean.

- March 24, 2000 to October 9, 2002, the burst of the dot.com bubble and the 9/11 terrorist attacks: minus 43.40%. From October 10, 2002 onward, annualized gains were: 1 year: 24.40%; 3 years: 16.72%; 5 years: 15.54%.
- July 17, 1998 to August 31, 1998, collapse of a major hedge fund: minus 19.30%, not quite a bear market. From September 1, 1998 onward, annualized gains were: 1 year: 39.82%; 3 years: 7.14%; 5

years: 2.48%; 10 years: 4.68%. All but the first year overlapped the next bear market.

- July 16, 1990 to October 11, 1990, energy cost spike when Iraq invades Kuwait sent the U.S into a recession. The market fell 20.10%. From October 12, 1990 onward, annualized gains were: 1 year: 31.16%; 3 years: 18.07%; 5 years: 17.23%; 10 years: 19.44%. The ten-year period overlapped another bear market.

- August 25, 1987 to December 4, 1987, minus 33.50%. On October 19, the S&P 500 Index dropped 20.4%. From December 5 onward, annualized gains were: 1 year: 23.33%; 3 years: 15.92%; 5 years: 17.30%; 10 years: 18.72%. The last two periods both overlapped bear markets.

- November 28, 1980 to August 12, 1982, major recession and high interest rates, the first recognized period of stagflation, minus 27.10%. From August 13 onward: 1 year: 59.26%; 3 years: 26.96%; 5 years: 29.63%; 10 years: 19.16%. The final period overlapped another bear market.

- January 11, 1973 to October 3, 1974, Watergate and Arab oil embargo, minus 48.20%. From October 4 onward, annualized gains were: 1 year: 38.14%; 3 years: 20.02%; 5 years: 16.86%; 10 years: 15.63%. The final period overlapped another bear market.

Just studying the record over the past 40 years shows there were six bear markets, an average of one in just over six years. The smallest loss was 19.30% and the largest was 48.20%. No one enjoyed those times and you will not either. But comfort yourself by looking at what happened after. The smallest gain in the following 12 months was 23.33%. The largest was 59.26%.

People who exited the market in panic at the end of the bear market locked in losses of 19.30% to 48.20%. Those losses could never be recovered; they were gone. And those people missed gains the following year of between 23.33% and 59.26%.

But that's not all. If you had saved regularly from your paycheck throughout each bear market you would have had the opportunity to invest at bargain-basement prices when everyone else was fleeing for the exits. You would have invested as the professionals do. The subsequent gains in your portfolio would have been even larger than those indicated by market performance.

Okay, so that's for markets as a whole, but what happens if you simply pick the wrong stock and the company goes bust? Don't you lose everything? Not if you keep in mind the principal of protecting capital and letting the profits take care of themselves. First of all, you should keep up with the news on a regular basis. There is no such thing as a surprise bankruptcy. News gets out; there is speculation in the press. If you do your homework you will see the signs fairly early. Will you lose money or have your profits reduced? Probably, but you will not put all your eggs in one basket by investing everything you have into a single stock.

Diversification

Diversification will save you. Some advisors recommend you should have about 20 different stocks; Warren Buffett suggests five to ten. But it's not just the numbers that are important; make sure that each stock is in a different industry. Don't invest in the automotive industry and cars at the same time. Different industrial groups move up or down in unison; some are more sensitive to interest rates than others; some rely more heavily on consumer attitudes than others.

If you have a properly diversified portfolio, a mistake in one selection will be made up by gains in others.

Continuing to build a war chest from your paycheck in falling markets, diversification and an understanding that recovery follows even the worst conditions should minimize the chances of panic and selling to lock in losses at the worst possible times.

If nothing else, remember this: The crowd is *always* wrong. Never follow the crowd. If it is panicking, it's time to buy, not to sell. If the crowd is in a feeding frenzy of buying, it's time to leave the party and protect your gains. When the office boy tells you he has just invested $100 in a penny stock and you should get in too, consider what you need to sell.

Knowing you can keep your nerve is one of the most important pieces of knowledge you can have. Without it you cannot be a millionaire investor. Even amazing luck will not do it; luck makes you think it will repeat indefinitely; it will not.

Chapter 14

Saving to Spend

W e haven't really discussed *why* you invest yet. It may seem to be a silly question. We all have a reason or maybe many reasons to want more money. Those reasons might include:

- College tuition
- Down payment on a home
- Starting a business
- Paying for a wedding
- Purchasing a car
- Taking a vacation
- Retiring comfortably

An unending list. There are even some people who invest as a hobby, as if investing were a competitive sport. In our view, that is something entirely different than the investing we're speaking about here. Investing is a business. It is carried out to make money, like any other business, and it needs to be approached in a businesslike manner.

But let's return to your investing program and why you undertake it. What we each do with our money is our decision and boils down to priorities. But what we spend money for and how we save for those expenditures can seriously affect the direction of our lives.

I will assume your top priority will be the costliest one - retirement. You do not need to become a millionaire employee to buy a car or to take an occasional vacation. But if you save incorrectly for such purchases you could ruin your chances of ever becoming a millionaire and using that money for larger goals that daily expenses and pleasures.

The Internal Revenue Service estimates that just three families of every 100 are self-supporting in retirement. The other 97 rely at least partially on Social Security, family, or friends. Just three had real freedom. At the time of the IRS study, real freedom meant accumulating net assets of just $575,000 by retirement. This is only half of the millionaire employee goal.

Many people simply started saving too late. Others used the wrong approach to saving and investing. A large percentage of those saving for retirement keep their money in CDs which we have already seen will not help them to achieve their goals. Hopefully you will not make these same mistakes now that you have read this book.

A 25-year-old who saves $200 a month and earns an average of 10% in gains and dividends can retire at age 65 with almost $1.2 million. Two hundred dollars a month is just $6.67 a day. How difficult is that if you have a reasonable job? Go back to the chapter on saving and track the cash that dribbles out of your pocket or purse unnoticed each day. You will probably be surprised by how easy it is to save $200 a month.

But if it is that easy, why are there so few millionaires? Starting late is the main reason. Time is far more important to the growth of your investments than the amount you save from your paycheck. Let's suppose your aim is to save $1 million from your paycheck alone and you begin on your 25th birthday with a plan to retire at age 65. You have 480 months to meet your goal. You would have to save $2,083.33 every month if your contribution was the only source of money. You would need to have a gigantic income to accomplish that.

But with tax-deferred growth of 10% using a 401(k) or IRA, the earning from your savings would outstrip the amount you contribute each year within just eight years. It will be almost six times higher within 20 years and 44 times high in your last year when you turn 65. Most of the money in the account comes from gains on your investments and dividends which you keep invested. It does not come directly from your paycheck.

But if you do not start this same savings program until you are age 30, the final value of the account at 65 will be a lot smaller. The difference in your contribution to the account is just $12,000. But what you really lost was 5 years of growth on the assets in the account. Those five years are worth more than 30 times the amount you put in. Because you started the same savings program 5 years later, the account at age 65 will be $453,000 smaller. Instead of $1.2 million, it will be just over $715,000. This is a huge difference—all triggered by the lack of time to grow.

Waiting until age 30 is easy to do. There are so competing demands for the money. You are eager to buy a car—the best car you can afford. Once out of college and earning a professional salary you may be eager to do some traveling, perhaps around the world. There are hundreds of gadgets, gizmos, and do-dads that you are hungry to get your hands on. Then just when you think you have everything under control you start to think about getting married, buying a house, and having children. There is always a very good and valid reason to put of saving to become a millionaire until later – much later.

This is exactly why only 3% of the population even makes it to the half-million dollar point. They spent the whole lives being busy buying what they want right now and not thinking at all about what they could have in ten, twenty, or thirty years.

The table below shows the vast difference between an investing plan that lasts 40 years and one that is shorter by 5 years, 10 years, or 15 years.

Table 14-1. Savings at $6.67 a day

Year End	Capital	Income at 10%	Total savings
1	2,400	240	2,640
5	14,652	1,465	16,117
10	38,250	3,825	42,075
15	76,254	7,625	83,879
20	137,460	13,746	151,206
25	236,033	23,603	259,636
30	394,786	39,479	434,264
35	650,458	65,046	715,504
40	1,062,222	106,222	1,168,444

Now let's see how important discipline is to your plans.

You have saved for 10 years. You have more than $42,000 in your investment account and you're feeling pretty good about that. You decide it's time to celebrate your achievement and take the family for a little vacation but you did not save separately for such an expense. You decide that taking $5,000 from the investment account will not affect it too much. After all, you are saving $2,400 so your net withdrawal is just $2,600. What harm can there be in that?

It turns out that the difference can be really huge. It is not the $5,000 that matters, but what that money can do over many years. The $5,000 step down in year 10 actually causes almost a $100,000 step down by year 40.

Table 14-2. Savings at $6.67 a day
with $5,000 withdrawn in Year 10

Year end	Capital	Income at 10%	Total savings
1	2,400	240	2,640
5	14,652	1,465	16,117
10	38,250	3,825	42,075
Spend $5,000 for vacation			37,075
15	68,933	6,893	75,827
20	125,670	12,567	138,237
25	217,045	21,705	238,750
30	364,206	36,421	400,627
35	601,210	60,121	661,331
40	982,907	98,291	1,081,197

You still make your million dollars but that single vacation, a net $2,600 from your investment account after 10 years, cost more than $87,000. How much would two or three 'treats' or a new car cost in that 40-year time-frame? Once you rationalize one expenditure, why not two? Or three? Or more? Where does it stop?

The answer is it must stop right here before you take a single penny from your retirement account for anything but retirement. There needs to be a separate investment or savings account for vacations, cars, children's tuition, emergencies and the rest of the list of expenses you will face during your working life.

College Tuition

We have already discussed the tax advantages for retirement accounts. There are also tax advantages for accounts set up to pay for the significant future expense of college tuition for children, if you have them.

Those who earn enough money to be active investors are the same people who make too much to qualify for college tuition grants and low interest loans. Since you can afford to invest, you are almost forced to also do so as a way to save for the college expenses your children will incur.

The financial industry and the government have created a number of investment vehicles specifically to help you manage this investment. States have created prepaid college tuition and 529 investment plans that can grow tax free if the money is used for college expenses. The odd name comes from the section of the IRS tax code under which these plans are created. They are available in every state and can be used for qualified education expenses at out-of-state colleges as well.

Contributions are not deductible but gains on investment are tax-free if used according to the IRS rules. As you can see from the savings tables above, if you start saving for a child's education early enough and invest wisely, income can quickly outstrip contributions. Add to this the fact that the government in a sense contributes to the cost of your child's education by not charging tax on the gains and this is a deal you cannot afford to miss.

There is extensive information on 529 investment plans on the web. One really useful site is: **http://www.savingforcollege.com/**

Prepaid tuition plans are another option. These allow you to freeze tuition costs at today's level by begin a savings plan now to pay for the tuition you will face years in the future. The state will use the money you give them now as an investment and in exchange will allow what you pay now to cover the tuition rates that your child will face in the future. You are effectively paying today's rates so your child can afford college in ten years. While they investments have a low risk of failing, they also provide a very small return on your investment. If you compare them to the performance of other alternatives you will find that they are about equal to the return on a CD over those same years. That is because the college system is using CD-like investments to grow the money to cover your future tuition. They are betting that they can grow it faster than the rate of college tuition grows.

The plans have a few limitations that you need to be aware of.
- They are intended for state residents only and must be used in the state of residence. Principal and interest will be unlikely to cover the full cost of tuition if your child decides to go to an out of state college where rates can be very different from your home state.
- There are stiff penalties if you wish to cancel the program, possibly including loss of all interest earned.
- There is a narrow definition of allowable expenses. Some plans allow only tuition. Room and board, course fees and books fall on the family's shoulders. Some will allow these expenses if there are excess tuition units or if tuition and fees are reduced by scholarships.

The more general 529 investment plan allows for investment in a range of mutual funds. It does not lock in today's tuition rates but should give a better average rate of return. Therefore, it is strictly a better option if you are disciplined enough to keep at it until your child is ready for college.

Remember that education and all other planned expenses should come out of a different pygg jar than that in which your retirement savings are kept.

Vacation

Saving for a vacation, birthday presents, or Christmas is something generally done on an annual basis. The time between expenditures is short. These savings should not be subjected to possible fluctuations of the stock market—unless you plan to disappoint your family at Christmas. A no-cost money market account that can be added to every month and withdrawn from on short notice is probably the best home for this money. It will pay slightly more than the bank. It might be a good idea to have a separate account for each purpose, then over spending in one area will not jeopardize others. It will serve to maintain discipline, too, when you know what each pot of gold is for and the real cost of not saving enough for your goal.

Automobile and Other Future Purchases

Cars are a slightly different kettle of fish. For one thing, most people do not buy a new one every year. And quite often dealers offer zero-interest options, especially late in the year.

There are two things to be considered here: the interest to be paid on a loan and the inflexibility of a loan. Once you take out a loan you are committed to regular payments no matter what. If you save to pay cash for your car, interest on your savings can help you pay for it. Over a four-year period the interest could pay for a fair amount of gas. If you run into difficulties, sickness in the family for example, you can easily delay the new purchase for a year or so while your money waits in the bank. It is difficult to do that with a loan unless it is insured through a bank. However, a bank loan will carry higher interest than a loan through a dealer specifically because of some of the added safety.

The stock market is not a good place to save for future purchases unless they are a long way off. When your children are born saving for their college tuition or a daughter's wedding are good examples of a long way off. Occasionally, the market will lose so badly that it takes 10 years or more to recover. You don't want that to happen the month before you pay for a wedding or the month before tuition is due. That is why these kinds of accounts usually shift their assets to cash as the event they are targeted for approaches.

Down Payment for a Home

Most banks today require least a 20% down payment from home buyers, a much larger amount than was required before the housing bubble burst. On a $250,000 home, that is $50,000. Offsetting this somewhat is the fact that house prices are now much lower and will probably remain so for as long as oversupply from repossessions continues. This may be a good time to buy a house since they near the bottom of their price cycle.

Most of us don't save $50,000 overnight. Saving $200 a month at 10% for about 12 years would do it. You could accomplish it in about 8½ years by saving $300 a month. With $500 a month it would only take six years. Or you could aim at a less expensive home to start with and move up from there later.

When it comes to paying off this debt and saving a ton of interest in the bargain, remember the tricks you learned in earlier chapters.

Saving to Start a Business

It is common knowledge that the vast majority of businesses fail in the first five years. Some are nothing more than a drain from the initial idea to the deathbed. Everyone who starts a business is sure their idea is so good they will be a millionaire in no time—just like those novice investors we learned about earlier. They also expect that the business will grow steadily over many years, without any ruinous disasters along the way.

Some good advice is to look after the losses and the profits will look after themselves. However certain you are of success, assume your idea will be a loser. Be prepared to lose money as well as time. Make sure your business venture is separated from your retirement and other savings. You don't want to tell your children they can't go to college because daddy screwed up. You don't want to face your wife and tell her your comfortable retirement has been washed away.

If you have to borrow money for your idea, make sure your personal assets are protected in the event something goes wrong. Most of all protect your IRA and 401(k). These are your future. Given the high risk of a business, do not assume *it* is your future until you have a track record worth believing in.

The list of things you are already saving for is long. If you want to start a business is there some way other than from your paycheck you can earn money to get started? What are you good at? Can you sell your knowledge as a consultant or writer? Do you have a hobby such as woodworking that would allow you to sell furniture? Could you bring in partners who would put up the money to back your idea? Could you sell the idea and let others run the business? Maybe your first business idea simply provides the seed money for your second idea. You can move from a small business to a larger one in the same way that people begin with a small house and move to up in later years.

The bottom line is that you need to be like a tiger protecting her cubs with respect to the savings you put aside for the things that are important to your family life. It is too easy to say, "Well, the business is important." But it is not important until there is real cash flowing in from it and into your bank account.

Downright Losses

An expenditure most people fail to consider is the unplanned loss of money. We have already seen too clearly that the stock market can deal some pretty savage blows. But, if you have that crystal ball that no one else can find, you will exit the stock market just as it reaches its high point and have sacks filled with cash to get back in again when it falls back to its low, which you will recognize accurately.

Nice fantasy, but nothing like the truth. However careful your research, there will be a surprise incident that sends markets spinning downward and you will be caught in the middle of it with everyone else. You cannot miss all the bumps in the road. But as you saw in the previous chapter, markets always come back and usually go on to new highs after a collapse.

There are a number of protective measures you can take. They include:
- Time
- Diversification
- Protective stop losses
- Portfolio rebalancing

- A monthly investment program
- Inflating your savings

Time

Markets have always recovered from economic and psychological ills but sometimes they take a while to do so. If you had invested $380 in the Dow Jones Industrial Average in August of 1929, you would have seen it dwindle to just $43 in June of 1932, a drop of more than 88%. It took until November 1954 to recover to that August 1929 level where you started with $380. Is it any wonder your grandparents who lived through this believe that stock market investing is not for the average citizen?

That recovery took over 25 years!

Statistics suggest that if you hold an investment grade common stock for only 1 year, there is a 70% chance of profit. Over 5 years, the odds of making a profit increase to 88%. A 10 year holding period offers a 96% chance.

As this is being written, the first decade of the 21st century shows every indication of being the worst 10-year period for the stock market in its almost 200-year history. Thanks to a pair of bear markets, stocks have lost an average of 0.5% each year. Even the mattress would have been a better place for your savings. This followed the 1990s when the average gain was 17.6%, the second-best gain in history behind the 1950s.

The average decline in the 1930s was 0.2%.

The good news is two-fold. Remember a while back we talked about valuation and price to earning ratios? Late in 1999, S&P 500 stocks traded at an all-time high of 44 times earnings (or P/E), which is more than double what most savvy investors recommend. It was a giant warning sign to get out of the market, but a warning sign that very few heeded.

The Standard & Poor 500 estimates a P/E of 19.93 by the end of 2010 and 17.19% by the end of 2011. These are much more reasonable levels.

Another piece of good news is that poor markets in the past have been followed by good markets. Typically, the worse the bad market, the better the good one that follows. The reverse is also true. The crashes of the 2000s followed the stellar growth of 1990s. Given the rarity of these kinds of 10-year losses, the odds are that good times lay ahead.

Protection

Having said that, it is essential to protect yourself in the stock market. You cannot just assume that because we have come through a long dry spell the roses will now come into full bloom. Even if all indicators are Green, you still need to move with caution. Do we need to repeat the message?

Protect against losses and profits will take care of themselves.

So, apart from the research we have recommended in earlier chapters, how do you ward off disaster and minimize the risk of the stock market being an unplanned expense?

We have already mentioned diversification as a way to reduce losses in a portfolio. A portfolio entirely invested in stocks can protect against one of those stocks taking an unexpected tumble, but what happens if the entire market declines? How do you protect yourself then? The answer is by diversifying into other assets.

As the stock market starts to get toppy and you begin to sell some stocks, move the money into bonds. Bonds move to some degree in the opposite direction to stocks. As smart investors move away from stocks while the mad horde is rushing in, much of their money flees to the relative safety of bonds. This influx of money pushes up bond prices.

But that is not all that's at work to move bond prices one way or the other. Bond prices take a parallel path to interest rates set by the Federal Reserve to deal with inflation and deflation. The Fed increases interest rates as the economy begins to grow from its previous low. Increased interest rates mean lower prices for existing bonds so, they can remain competitive with the new bonds that carry higher rates (see earlier chapter).

While this is taking place, the stock market—with a few bumps along the way—is generally moving higher and you make good profits from your stocks. As the economy continues to grow and your shares move ever higher, the Fed gradually moves rates higher to ward off economic overheating and inflation.

At some point, bond market rates force serious investors to start to pay attention. Price/earning ratios are high, interest rates are high and the "crazy crowd" is scrambling to buy any stock on the horizon. You will also notice an increase in the number of new stock issues, particularly speculative stock, as companies scramble to sell themselves to investors at very high P/E levels. Many companies will buy these same shares back at bargain prices once the market falls, making a huge profit while the people who bought their stock when it was too high are going broke.

This is a good time to flee to cash. It is not yet time for bonds. The stock market tries to guess economic conditions about nine months ahead, so when it tops out, interest rates are usually still on the rise. Not too long after the market turns south, the economy begins to weaken. And when that happens, the Fed starts to reduce rates to avoid a recession. It's like a car being driven up and down a series of steep hills. In one direction, there's a need for more gas and a heavier foot on the accelerator—in the form of low interest rates. At other times, the brakes are needed to slow it down—in the form of higher interest rates.

If the Fed is too heavy on the gas, they risk causing inflation; if it steps too hard on the brakes, they risk a recession. It is a very difficult balancing act and obviously the Fed gets it wrong from time to time. But when interest rates fall while stocks are still falling the price of bonds increases and holders of bonds have an opportunity to make capital gains on top of the interest they receive.

In a perfect world, you would know exactly when to move from stocks to cash to bonds. In case you had not noticed, this isn't a perfect world. To protect against market extremes, many investors hold a mixture of stocks, bonds and cash in the form of money market funds. They allow the fund manager to do this balancing act for them, for a small price.

The degree to shift from stock to bonds or cash depends on your age. A younger investor can afford to ignore market declines if his stomach can stand them. Younger investors have time on their side and any temporary losses will be made up in the future. Older investors need to be more cautious and should have a greater leaning toward bonds and cash. But that does not mean they should forgo growth entirely. Yesterday's old person is today's middle age. At 65 many investors still have another 20 years ahead of them. You do not want to spend those 20 years with all of your money in cash when you could be earning much larger gains with the portion that you will not be needing for another 5 years.

Rebalancing

A diversified stock portfolio in the course of a year during a bull market will see some stocks rise, some stay roughly the same and some fall. Assuming that all are good healthy companies and each is in an industry removed from all the others, there is a way to always buy at lower prices and sell at higher ones. Just this act will move you to greater ongoing safety.

The method requires that at the start of a year you have an equal amount of cash in each stock. At the end of the year, you total the value of the entire portfolio and divide that number by the number of stocks you hold. You sell some of those having a value greater than the average and use the proceeds to buy more of those that are undervalued.

Let's look at part of a larger portfolio to show how this works. $1,000 was invested in each of these stocks on December 31, 2008, while the bear market was scaring the socks off everyone but when you, using the tools in this book, may have been buying.

Table 14-3. Investments in Solid Companies with Growth Ahead

Company	Original purchase price	Recent price	Number of shs held	Recent value
Caterpillar Inc.	$44.67	56.99	25.8352	1,472.35
Diana Shipping	$12.76	14.48	85.7007	1,240.95
Freeport-McMoRan	$24.44	80.29	43.2166	3,469.86
Goldman Sachs	$84.39	168.84	12.6858	2,141.87
The Home Depot	$23.02	28.93	49.4263	1,429.90
Intel Corp	$14.66	20.40	74.3372	1,516.48

Each month during 2009, $10 was added to each stock as both a saving and a protective measure we will discuss next. As you can see, the results varied. Goldman Sachs share value was twice what it was one year earlier. Freeport was worth more than three times as much. Diana Shipping had not moved much. The original investment in these six stocks was $6,000. During the year, $720 in new savings was added. Value of this portion of the portfolio totaled $11,271.41 at the end of the year. Divide this number by the six stocks and you get a rounded number of $1,878.57.

This is what the value of each holding needed to be after a little buying and selling. You sell part of the holding of every stock valued above this and use the proceeds to bring up the worth of each that is lower than this figure. Automatically, over time you buy at a relatively low price and sell at a relatively high one.

Now, this sample portfolio paid no commissions. If you want to minimize commissions, you can simply stop adding money to those that are overpriced and focus on those that are underpriced. This is not necessarily a better deal than selling stocks that have appreciated because you miss out on capturing the profits from those. But it is an alternative that you should be aware of.

> **BUYING WITHOUT COMMISSIONS**
> Something no broker will tell you is that there are approximately 1,000 companies whose stocks trade in the U.S that will allow you to buy their stock with zero commission, even to fractions of shares as if they were individual mutual funds. Each company has its own rules for setting up an account. The Moneypaper Inc.'s Guide to Direct Investment Plans, an annual publication, is essential reading if you wish to go this route. By now, you should realize we are on the side of penny pinchers. This is another way to pinch pennies and add to your retirement nest egg.

Dollar Cost Averaging

Here's another way to protect yourself and, in fact, make some extra profit in a falling market. Dollar cost averaging is just a fancy term for investing regular amounts of money each month. You will probably do this with your 401(k) plan already. Mutual funds are an ideal vehicle for it. Let's look at a fictional scenario so you can more easily see how it can work in your favor in a falling market.

Let's assume you invest $100 a month to keep the math simple. Your mutual fund units are $27 when you begin right at the start of a bear market. Your investment buys 3.7 units that month. But, oh no! Over the next month the shares have dropped by $1. You are stubborn and invest another $100 the following month. The price is now $26 and you are able to buy 3.85 units, just a little more because the price is lower. But your *average* price for all of the shares you own is now $26.49. The shares continue to slide, right down to $18. By this time, you have invested $1,300. If you had invested the whole amount at the beginning your little nest egg would have fallen in value to a mere $866.67. You would have lost one-third and your spouse might make you sleep on the couch.

But dollar cost averaging reduced that loss to $296.69 instead of $433.33. And that's not all. When the shares struggled back up to where they started, your friend who put all his money in up front breathed a large sigh of relief, took his money and ran so he would not be exposed to the same experience again. He had a lot of anxiety and made no profit to compensate for that. You, on the other hand, had a profit of $511.96. All you had to do was stick with the plan with the knowledge that when the market righted itself you would be at far better than break even. You would have been breaking even when the share price rose to a fraction over $22.

Table 14-4. Effective Dollar Cost Averaging

Dollar Cost Averaging					
Price of Shares	Shares bought at $100	Total shares owned	Average price	Total invested	Total value
27	3.70	3.70	27.00	100.00	100.00
26	3.85	7.55	26.49	200.00	196.30
25	4.00	11.55	25.97	300.00	288.75
24.5	4.08	15.63	25.59	400.00	382.97
24	4.17	19.80	25.25	500.00	475.16
25	4.00	23.80	25.21	600.00	594.95
26	3.85	27.64	25.32	700.00	718.75
25	4.00	31.64	25.28	800.00	791.11
24	4.17	35.81	25.13	900.00	859.46
23	4.35	40.16	24.90	1,000.00	923.65
21	4.76	44.92	24.49	1,100.00	943.33
19	5.26	50.18	23.91	1,200.00	953.49
18	5.56	55.74	23.32	1,300.00	1,003.31
18	5.56	61.29	22.84	1,400.00	1,103.31
20	5.00	66.29	22.63	1,500.00	1,325.90
20.5	4.88	71.17	22.48	1,600.00	1,459.05
20	5.00	76.17	22.32	1,700.00	1,523.46
21.5	4.65	80.82	22.27	1,800.00	1,737.72
22	4.55	85.37	22.26	1,900.00	1,878.13
22.5	4.44	89.81	22.27	2,000.00	2,020.82
22	4.55	94.36	22.26	2,100.00	2,075.91
23	4.35	98.71	22.29	2,200.00	2,270.27
23.5	4.26	102.96	22.34	2,300.00	2,419.62
24	4.17	107.13	22.40	2,400.00	2,571.10
25	4.00	111.13	22.50	2,500.00	2,778.23
26	3.85	114.98	22.61	2,600.00	2,989.36
26.5	3.77	118.75	22.74	2,700.00	3,146.85
26	3.85	122.60	22.84	2,800.00	3,187.48
26.5	3.77	126.37	22.95	2,900.00	3,348.77
27	3.70	130.07	23.06	3,000.00	3,511.96

Inflating Your Saving

We have touched on this subject earlier. It is almost unavoidable. A healthy economy has a certain amount of inflation but, like hot peppers, not too much.

Since inflation is a given, we need to look at it like any other expense. Most people planning their retirement don't know how to account for it or to have their savings purchase what they forecast years ahead of time. Here's a simple way to get around the potential problem: Long term, inflation has averaged 3%. Simply add $3 to every $100 you save and do this every year. You save $100 in the first year, $103 in the second year, $106.09 in the third year and so on. Salary increases will surely make up for the additional savings so they should not put any additional strain on your budget.

These are just a few of the tricks that experienced investors have learned to use to make the most of what they are able to save.

Chapter 15

Where Do We Go
From Here?

We've come a long way. You have become a millionaire and you thought all your problems would be solved. Instead, you have found a new set of problems. Luckily these are better problems than being poor and in debt. So let's work on them together.

What do people want after good health and a loving family? The answer is almost always freedom. Money gives you that to some extent. Have enough of it and within the bounds of law, decency, and ability you can do almost anything you want when you want. But you have also gained a responsibility that you never had before.

Let's suppose you own a business that has dozens of excellent workers who, because of the dedication and training they bring to their jobs, bring you wealth that you could not achieve alone. You would do everything you could to look after and to protect those workers? You actually have workers like this. They are Money Workers. All of those dollars that you put to work around the clock to earn more than you make from your regular job; those dollars are your workers.

Your Money Workers never ask for a vacation, never call in sick, and don't demand vacation days... but they are lazy. That's their one weakness. You have to tell them what to do. Leave them alone and they are like children without direction; they will sit in a bank, lounging around in hammocks, doing absolutely nothing. Fortunately, you have learned how to put them to work profitably and you have been successful at keeping them safe from various dangers most of the time.

But there are others who see what a great job your well-trained and managed Money Workers have done for you and they want them for themselves. They skulk around wondering and plotting how to steal them from you. The more wealth you gain the more you recognize the need to protect what you have worked so hard to achieve. But what will happen to all this wealth when you are no longer around to manage it or spend it?

None of us live forever and it would be amazing if we expired from natural causes on the exact day we spent our last penny. So who will benefit from our careful efforts? Topping the list will most likely be the spouse who has supported you with encouragement while you built those pennies into dollars. What about children or grandchildren? Are any still in need of a good education? Are there charities or a church you want to help? Do you want your Money Workers to keep out of their hammocks and continue to be productive, and if so who will best manage them? How can you spare the greatest number of Money Workers from the inhuman clutches of the IRS?

You need at least some of the following helpers:

- Tax accountant
- Family lawyer
- Will
- Guide for those managing your estate
- Conservator
- Living trust

Accountant

Accountants come in a variety of shapes and colors. You need one who specializes in tax matters and who can advise you on how to arrange your affairs long before your eventual demise.

Estate taxes in 2010 were levied on amounts above $3.5 million but that limit is scheduled to come to an end unless the government extends it. As things stand at the time of writing, just the first $1 million will escape tax from 2011 onward but with a government desperately in need of money who can say how long that will last. You already have $1 million. And a house. And insurance. And what else? Your tax accountant will help you to protect your Money Workers.

Family Lawyer

You need this specialist to help you to draw up a will to divide your major assets in the way you want them distributed. Give some thought to the broad division of assets early in your life, as soon as you have assets worth dividing. If you fail to do this and die without a will the state will appoint an administrator who will divvy up the spoils according to his or her view of how things should be. This will not necessarily be how you and your family would have wanted it done.

Your lawyer should be able to help your family avoid probate court, a lengthy and costly legal procedure. Among other things, make sure at least one of your bank accounts is held jointly with your spouse. He or she will have immediate access to it for those many expenses when you die. It would not make sense if you have $1 million in investments and your family is going hungry for months during the probate process.

Each state has its own laws so you probably want to make sure your family lawyer operates in your state of residency.

Will

Your will should be simple, covering just the main points. It may be just a single page. The minuscule details and messages to Aunt Sue should be saved for another and less formal document we will discuss in a minute. If your will is too complicated it will need to be changed every time there is a relatively minor change in your circumstances. Keep it to the bare bones and you will not only save the expense of redoing it but it will be closer to what is really needed when the time comes for its use.

Your will appoints an executor, the person tasked with seeing that the details of your will are carried out according to your wishes. My strong advice is that you also appoint a backup. In one real case, when an elderly woman suffering from Alzheimer's died, her only surviving relatives were a young nephew and his wife. The woman was believed to have a considerable sum of money in England but no one knew how much or where. The woman had appointed an executor but the executor had died before the aunt and the aunt was not mentally competent to appoint another. As a result, the estate entered probate court, paid for those expenses, and settlement was delayed for months. This could have been avoided if she had just appointed her nephew as an alternative executor when she created her will.

Estate Management Guide

A good estate management guide will help your executor and relatives to avoid making mistaken assumptions about your final plans. Decisions which may seem obvious when the person is healthy and not quite so clear when they have passed away. Some details that need to be covered in the guide are:

- *Physician.* Who is it and how can they be contacted?
- *Clergy.* Who should preside at the funeral?
- *Funeral Director.* Who would you like to provide your funeral arrangements?
- *Family Members.* Do you have a list of all family members who should be notified of your death, along with their contact information?
- *Friends and Associates.* Do you have a list of friends who should be notified?
- *Safe Deposit Box.* Where is it located and where is the key stored?
- *Will.* Where is your will located? Is it with a lawyer or a relative?
- *Storage.* Do you have a rented storage space somewhere and if so where is the key?

Where do you keep things for safekeeping?

Every year in communities across the country the locks of dormant safety deposit boxes are drilled and their contents removed for disposal. The owner forgot to leave a record of where the key was kept. A completed estate management guide could have prevented this small annoyance and cost, as well as dozens of similar problems.

Your estate management guide should contain the answers to all of the questions above and many more which are unique to you.

Think of what survivors will have to do. This document should be designed to take away as uncertainty and work as possible. Remember, close relatives will not be at the top of their mental game in the days after you are gone. Do your best to help them now when everything is thinking clearly.

Conservator

Conservators are usually appointed by the courts, but we use the term loosely here to describe a role rather than a legal definition.

Here's what we have in mind:
- When you die, you have $1 million invested
- These investments are kicking out $100,000 a year in gains
- Your spouse knows nothing about investing

What is the best course of action? If the investments are liquidated and the money moved to a bank account or some hands-off investment vehicle it is unlikely to provide the same degree of income. You don't want to trust the future welfare of your family to a professional who has no vested interest other than fees and commissions. But perhaps you have a long-time family friend or relative who is a successful investor.

You might want to appoint this person as an informal conservator to look after your investments and ensure they continue to produce a healthy return.

This is not a decision to be taken lightly. You need to discuss it and your choice with your spouse first and get full agreement on this idea and this person. Make sure you explain all the risks and the options so your spouse can offer an informed opinion; it is his or her future that is at stake here.

The person you ask to be your informal conservator should have clear guidelines from you regarding your portfolio, or business if you have one. Don't put all the risk or blame on his shoulders if something goes wrong. You should probably formalize an agreement and pay this person an honorarium based on his performance.

Living Trust

There is currently one lawyer for every 210 people in the United States. That's more than one for every 100 families. No wonder there are so many law suits. With so much competition, lawyers have to find a way to make a living. One way they do this is by dreaming up ways to file lawsuits against the estates of the recently deceased.

You never had to worry about this when you started out, but now you do. If you drive a nice car, or live in a nice house in a nice area, you are assumed to have money. You don't need to live the flashy lifestyle. If you have money there are others who want it—it's that simple and that harsh.

The easy way to avoid your Money Workers being kidnapped is not to have any. Give them away! But, I can hear you ask as if you think I have lost my marbles, why would I go to all the trouble of accumulating them just to give them away? It's simple, you give them away to a living trust you still control during your life. You and your family get all the benefit of the Money Workers but they now work for you from a different address.

Your house, your boat, your car, your investments, anything of value belongs to your living trust. You still live in the house, still sail the boat and drive the car, your wife still wears her favorite jewelry. But when the lawyer for Mr. Avarice calls with a notice of intent to sue for all the money he thinks you have, he will quickly fade away into the bushes when he discovers that you, personally, are broke.

Your trust legally owns everything but you maintain control of everything just as you did before you relinquished ownership. Mr. Avarice cannot sue a trust in the normal course of events other than for a legal debt.

A living (or inter vivos) trust also:
- Avoids probate that can take months and eat up some 5% of the value of an estate in legal and court fees. Ownership is simply transferred to those named in the trust.
- Is fairly simple to set up and is not much more complicated than a will. You can make one yourself with the help of books such as *Make Your Own Living Trust* by attorney Denis Clifford.
- Is never made public, but a will is.
- Does not do away with the need for a will. A will is an essential backup document for property you do not transfer to yourself as trustee of a trust.
- A simple living trust for the purpose of eliminating probate will not reduce estate taxes, but a more complicated version can reduce them greatly for those with a lot of valuable assets. One tax-saving trust is designed primarily for couples with children. Each spouse leaves property to the other in trust for life and then to the children. The tax saving could be hundreds of thousands of dollars, money that will be passed on to the couple's final inheritors.

Life Has Been Good

You have worked hard to get this far, your loved ones are secure and protected, but is there anything else?

Many successful people for whatever reason, religious or otherwise, believe they should pass on some of their good fortune to others less fortunate. Some establish scholarships or donate money for public buildings or the arts. There is no end to what you can do with money not needed by your family.

If you want a tax advantage, though, make sure the recipient organization is a registered charity in the meaning of the tax code.

One piece of good news: you are not required to die to give money to a good cause.

There are some benefits to setting up a charitable trust, but you'll need at least $50,000. Banks probably will not bother with less than $1 million. The amount depends on the manager. Universities will happily accept $50,000. Some private foundation services will not set up a charitable trust for less than $500,000.

If you consider setting up this type of trust you should know you cannot change your mind. You need to be sure before you even consider such a move that your family is taken care of no matter what happens. Even if they are starving, they cannot get a single red cent from this type of trust.

In some ways, unless you have a lot more than just one million dollars, it may be better simply to make out a check to your favorite charity or leave them money in your will.

◆ ◆ ◆

There's no such thing as total freedom. Money carries its own responsibilities. But having it is far better than not having it.

Chapter 16

Getting and Staying Educated

Invest in stocks, bonds, real estate, collectibles or other items of value and you participate in the daily growth and change of society. This makes you an active part of a dynamic system of money, people and organizations. Understanding this system is a constant challenge. The world does not stand still; it is not static. Rather, it is a dynamic, rational, irrational, and emotional system with billions of moving parts.

No single person or even the most advanced computers can understand it all. Everyone does their best to keep up with the changes in their small part of the world. Books, magazines, newspapers, newsletters, Web sites, television and radio all do their best to capture and condense essential information and deliver it to consumers.

The Millionaire Employee Investor has to be immersed in this stream of information. You have to find one hour a day to read, listen, and stay informed about the changes in the world. Since you are also an employee working a full-time job, the amount of time you have to spend in the information stream is much more limited than those who invest for a living. You cannot read and watch everything. You will have to be selective.

Moreover, each information format has a different characteristic. Let's review a few of them.

Books

In the beginning, books will be your most important source of information. As you get started, you have very limited knowledge and experience. Most books are written to help you build a foundation from which you can transition to more current sources of knowledge.

Because of the preparation time, they describe the past. Once published, a book may remain in print and be accessible for decades. By necessity, these books talk about the world as it was in the past. Most books present information as either a fundamental and constant part of the world going forward; or as a historical lesson that may be instructive in understanding why things happen in the future.

During my career, I have read hundreds of books on investing and making money. Many of these are still piled on my office bookshelves. Every time my family packed the house to move to a new home or to a new state, I sifted through the books, kept those worth keeping and got rid of those that had to find another home.

The books listed in this section are relatively current and available. Among all of these, two provided me with excellent guidance in handling my investments.

In 1986, when I was fresh out of graduate school and just beginning to study investing, I picked up a copy of Andrew Tobias' *The Only Investment Guide You will Every Need*. It was my first real introduction to investing and it had a big influence on my decision to get into the stock market via mutual funds. That little book gave me the confidence to break away from the bank savings account, open a brokerage account, and begin investing.

My parents had kept their life savings in bank savings accounts and in certificates of deposit. This was the investment pattern they passed down to me, and it is the investment pattern they have stuck with. But Tobias' book encouraged me to look beyond the local bank and to invest in the growth of American businesses through the stock market.

I also remember a piece of advice Tobias wrote for Money magazine's annual "What to do with $1,000?" article. He advised readers to take their $1,000 and invest it in one share of a company I had never heard of – Berkshire Hathaway. I thought buying one share of stock with a price of $1,000 was a crazy idea and of course I ignored the advice. Twenty-five years later, I remember that advice and wish I had listened. Berkshire Hathaway shares are now trading for more than $100,000.

Much later in my investment career, I discovered an old book on selecting stocks based on their long-term value rather than their potential for immediate growth. Prior to that, I was playing the stock market with little more knowledge than someone playing blackjack in Las Vegas. The book is Benjamin Graham's *The Intelligent Investor*. Graham and many others who follow his ideas suggest that since a stock is a piece of a real company, you should select those you buy as if you were buying the whole company and will be sticking with it for years to come.

Graham's book helps to illustrate the difference between speculating in a stock for its immediate growth and investing in a company for its long-term growth. Everyone investing in the stock market should read Graham's book. My edition has been annotated with commentary by Jason Zweig, and his modern explanations of Graham's ideas are worth reading.

Hundreds of good books exist on investing and creating wealth, and dozens are listed here. Reading the two mentioned above is a good way for anyone to get started. Others worthy of your attention include:

Bach, David. (2005) *The Automatic Millionaire Homeowner: A Powerful Plan to Finish Rich in Real Estate*. Broadway Books.

Browne, Christopher. (2007) *The Little Book of Value Investing*. John Wiley & Sons.

Cohen, Marilyn. (2000) *The Bond Bible*. New York Institute of Finance.

Cramer, Jim. (2006) *Jim Cramer's Mad Money: Watch TV, Get Rich*. Simon & Schuster.

Graham, B. (1996) *The Intelligent Investor: A Book of Practical Counsel*. HarperCollins Publishers.

Green, E. (1989) *Banking: An Illustrated History*. Rizzoli Publishers.

Hagstrom, Robert. (1994) *The Warren Buffet Way: Investment Strategies of the World's Greatest Investor*. John Wiley & Sons.

Hagstrom, Robert. (1999) *The Warren Buffet Portfolio: Mastering the Power of the Focus Investment Strategy*. John Wiley & Sons.

Kennedy, Diane & Sutton, Garrett. (2003) *Real Estate Loop-holes: Secrets of Successful Real Estate Investing*. Warner Books.

Kiyosaki, Robert. (2000) *Guide to Investing: What the Rich Invest In, That the Poor and Middle Class Do Not*. Warner Books.

Means, H. (2001) *Money & Power: The History of Business*. John Wiley & Sons.

Thomsett, Michael. (2008) *Winning with Options: The Smart Way to Manage Portfolio Risk and Maximize Profit.* American Management Association.

Tobias, A. (2005) *The Only Investment Guide You'll Ever Need.* Harvest Books.

Town, Phil. (2006) *Rule #1: The Simple Strategy for Successful Investing in Only 15 Minutes a Week.* Crown Publishers.

Zipf, Robert. (1997) *How the Bond Market Works.* New York Institute of Finance.

Every author has built upon the works of others. There are easily thousands of books on investing available to you. The above list includes some of my favorites, and you have many others to choose from. You will need to make your own path through them; I am just getting you started on that path.

Periodicals

Newspapers provide a more current picture of the economy, the market, and society and attempt to capture information relevant for several weeks or months. Monthly magazines contain information that is dated and provide a picture of the past.

Periodicals are good sources for tapping into the ideas and advice of columnists who summarize current situations and review books you do not have time to read. Magazines are useful for entry-level investors still developing their big picture of the world. I recommend the following periodicals for entry-level investors.

Money Magazine
Smart Money

Both are well written and attempt to provide high-level coverage on a variety of investment concepts and investing.

As you move into intermediate levels of investing, you need to stay abreast of what's going on and have access to more current and more detailed information. You can usually find such information in financial newspapers, such as the following.

Wall Street Journal
Barron's Weekly
Good Local Newspapers

Web Sites

There was a time when daily newspapers provided the most current information available. But that changed with the commercialization of the Internet. Today, the Internet provides information within minutes of its occurrence.

You can track the status of investments and world events in near real time. Google, Yahoo!, and MSN have each done admirable jobs of presenting financial information. Your brokerage company also maintains a wealth of information to help you evaluate potential investments and to execute the trades that you decide to make.

Finding a good investment club and becoming a member can be a useful idea. Just make sure you find one in which the members are more serious about investing and less about socializing. The advantage of a good investment club is that research and the results of that research are shared among all the members.

But there are some drawbacks. As a requirement, investment clubs are filled with active participants. From researching stocks and companies to seeking out asset management software and recruiting new members to the group, they are not only a sink of money but also of time. You need to have the patience to read the fine print on everything, from your club's charter to its bylaws and policies regarding duties. You also need to be able to read articles about stocks, hunt down information about other companies on the Internet, and generally be willing to contribute pertinent and useful tidbits to the club.

Granted, this isn't necessarily a bad thing. If you actually have the free time to attend the meetings and perform your duties as stated in the contract you'll sign.

If there isn't a club in your area, then start one! You can find help on starting one of these clubs at: **http://www.investmentclubhelp.com/**

As you read more information on investing and tap into other information sources, you will learn, grow, shift, and change constantly. You will never have a shortage of new information to explore. Just remember you are seeking an understanding of your investment options. Do not get lost in a sea of information and forget why you are even looking at it.

www.ingramcontent.com/pod-product-compliance
Lightning Source LLC
Chambersburg PA
CBHW021033210326
41598CB00016B/1005